ADVANCED QUESTIONS ON

EVERYDAY

PHYSICS

WITH ANSWERS

Susan Williams

Nelson Blackie

Thomas Nelson and Sons Ltd
Nelson House Mayfield Road
Walton-on-Thames Surrey
KT12 5PL UK

51 York Place
Edinburgh
EH1 3JD UK

Nelson Blackie
Wester Cleddens Road
Bishopbriggs
Glasgow
G64 2NZ UK

Thomas Nelson (Hong Kong) Ltd
Toppan Building 10/F
22A Westlands Road
Quarry Bay Hong Kong

Thomas Nelson Australia
102 Dodds Street
South Melbourne
Victoria 3205 Australia

Nelson Canada
1120 Birchmount Road
Scarborough Ontario
M1K 5G4 Canada

First published by Thomas Nelson and Sons Ltd 1993

ISBN 0-17-448203-5
NPN 9 8 7 6 5 4 3 2 1

Printed in Great Britain by Bell and Bain Ltd., Glasgow

ACKNOWLEDGEMENTS

The authors and publishers wish to thank the following sources for permission to reproduce the material indicated.

Photographic material
Allsport: p 6
F. Gibson Photography: p 10
Andrew Lambert: pp 14, 22, 38, 53, 85
Rolls Royce plc: p 15
Science Photo Library: pp 21, 23, 25, 27, 36, 51, 57, 83

Articles and advertisements
William Leven Ltd: p 1
Vauxhall Motors Ltd: p 2
The Guardian: pp 6, 7
Felix Magazine: p 18
New Scientist: pp 29, 30, 47, 72, 73, 79
Innovations Magazine: pp 49, 88 (left and right)
Sony (UK) Limited: p 56
Electricity Association: p 59
Electronics World and Wireless World: p 63
Radiodetection Ltd: p 65, 67
High Magazine: p 69, 70
Natural History Museum: p 76
Panasonic (UK) Limited: p 81

INTRODUCTION

Advanced Questions on Everyday Physics is divided into four sections:

- mechanics;
- wave motion;
- electricity, fields and electromagnetism;
- matter.

Within these sections there are a number of stimulus items such as newspaper articles and magazine advertisements with accompanying context-based questions. The questions involve the reader in: discussing the implications of discoveries, solving problems based on physical principles, estimating quantities and predicting outcomes.

A full set of answers is also provided at the back of the book.

CONTENTS

The figures in brackets denote the page number on which the corresponding answers to questions can be found.

MECHANICS

WAVE MOTION

ELECTRICITY, FIELDS AND ELECTROMAGNETISM

MATTER

MECHANICS

1 ▶ AN OPENING PROBLEM OF SOME MOMENT

Look at the advertisement and photographs about the *Magitwist* jar and bottle opener and then answer the questions which follow.

FACT FILE

$T = F \times d$ where T = torque in Nm, F = force in N and d = the perpendicular distance in m of the line of action of the force from the axis of rotation.

1 The round rubber grip is made of slightly sticky rubber. Why does this help the action of the opener?

2 Draw a diagram showing the forces acting when the opener is in use. Explain why this opener is of particular use to disabled or elderly people who have developed a weak grip. Support your answer with estimated calculations.

3 A vinegar bottle has a screwtop of diameter 3 cm. A jam-jar has a screwtop of diameter 8 cm done up to the same 'degree of tightness'.
  a) What do you think is meant by the phrase *degree of tightness*?
  b) If the same frictional force is exerted by the black stopper on each container, show by calculation which one, if either, will be easier to open when the opener is used.
  c) Is the opener more effective on smaller or larger tops?

4 In industry, items which are difficult to unscrew are sometimes opened by wrapping a chain round them and pulling.
  a) Why is this effective?

b) What disadvantages does this method have when compared to the *Magitwist* opener?

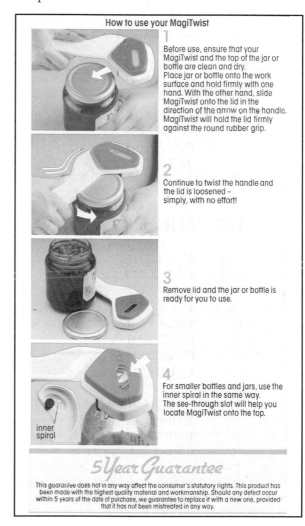

How to use your MagiTwist

1 Before use, ensure that your MagiTwist and the top of the jar or bottle are clean and dry.
Place jar or bottle onto the work surface and hold firmly with one hand. With the other hand, slide MagiTwist onto the lid in the direction of the arrow on the handle. MagiTwist will hold the lid firmly against the round rubber grip.

2 Continue to twist the handle and the lid is loosened – simply, with no effort!

3 Remove lid and the jar or bottle is ready for you to use.

inner spiral

4 For smaller bottles and jars, use the inner spiral in the same way. The see-through slot will help you locate MagiTwist onto the top.

5 Year Guarantee

This guarantee does not in any way affect the consumer's statutory rights. This product has been made with the highest quality material and workmanship. Should any defect occur within 5 years of the date of purchase, we guarantee to replace it with a new one, provided that it has not been mistreated in any way.

Read the advertisement about Vauxhall cars
and then answer the questions which follow.

4x4=GRIP.

H396 XYL

F434 PUL

By now, most people know that 4-wheel drive systems clamp you to the road. The Cavalier 4-wheel drive system is no exception.

Where it parts company with ordinary 4-wheel drive, though, is that it has brains as well as brawn.

By constantly monitoring the speed of each wheel, the system adjusts the power transmission between front and rear drive-shafts.

Up a steep gravel incline, for instance, it would split the torque as much as 40/60 in favour

of the rear wheels. The same goes for icy roads, or muddy terrain. (This 4x4 is a confirmed mudlark.)

Under 'normal' driving conditions, the split changes in favour of the front wheels (100% in favour, if necessary) and you get what is, in effect, front wheel drive. As you do during sudden braking.

Because, in a fifth of a second, the rear drive is electronically disconnected, which allows the ABS to bring the car to a safe and stable halt.

In other words, it's a 4-wheel drive system that

gives you as much or as little 4-wheel drive as you need, as and when you need it.

Like all Vauxhalls, the Cavalier 4x4 is covered by Vauxhall Assistance, our unique roadside recovery and accident management service.

And by Price Protection, our promise that the price you're quoted is the price you pay if you agree to take delivery within 3 months of order.

To see the Cavalier with 'intelligent 4-wheel drive', sports trim, sports wheels, updated interior

and the 130bhp version of the famous 2.0i Cavalier engine, try your local Vauxhall dealer.

You'll be transported. THE CAVALIER 4x4

VAUXHALL
Once driven, forever smitten.

*F*ACT FILE

For a body to be in equilibrium (i) the resultant force on it must be zero and (ii) the total torque about any axis is zero.
$T = F \times d$ where T = torque in N m, F = force in N and d = the perpendicular distance in m of the line of action of the force from the axis.

1 The advertisers sponsoring this photograph presumably want the observer to imagine that the tyres of the car are firmly gripping the road. Assuming that the photograph is genuine and that the position shown is stable, explain why no such gripping effect is necessary.

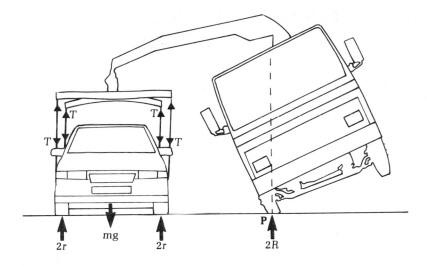

Fig. 2.1

2 Assuming that the mass of the van is eight times that of the crane and that you can treat the overhead crane as a uniform beam (see Fig.2.1), estimate:

a) the position of the centre of mass of the van and crane system.

b) the position of the centre of mass of the car.

3 a) Assuming that the van and crane system has twice the mass of the car, estimate:

  i) the clockwise moment of the weight of the van and crane system about the point P.

  ii) the anticlockwise moment of the weight of the car about the point P.

b) Do you think the system is stable as shown? If so, why?

4 Assuming that the situation is stable, the mass of the car is m and the tension in each of the four links from the crane to the car is T, as shown in Fig.2.1,

a) what will be the value of T if the crane and van alone are perfectly balanced?

b) what will be the value of T if the car is just about to leave the ground?

c) what are the possible maximum and minimum values of the tension T ?

5 If the reaction at each car wheel is r, the reaction at each van wheel touching the ground is R and the situation is in equilibrium, write down equations showing the relationship between the forces acting on:

a) the car.

b) the van and crane system.

(Hint: use a free-body diagram for each.)

6 Calculate the maximum and minimum value of the total reaction at P.

7 Why is four-wheel drive useful in variable driving conditions?

3 ▶ DANGEROUS TIMES

Small caterpillars crawl under leaves when heavy rain falls. It isn't that they just want to keep dry, they also need to avoid the devastating blow of a direct hit from a rain drop, which could prove fatal.

FACT FILE

Impulse = change in momentum or
$F \times t = mv - mu$

Kinetic energy = $\frac{1}{2}mv^2$

Potential energy = mgh

$v = u = at$

$v^2 = u^2 + 2as$

$s = ut + \frac{1}{2}at^2$

$F = ma.$

1 A large drop of rain is falling vertically. It strikes a stationary caterpillar, of mass 1 g, on the edge of a leaf. Calculate the force exerted on the caterpillar if the drop is in contact with the caterpillar for 0.1 ms and the caterpillar moves off, as a result of the impact, with a speed of 2 m s⁻¹.

2 If a gale is blowing, a drop of rain could strike the same caterpillar so that the caterpillar leaves the leaf with a horizontal velocity of 0.5 m s⁻¹. If the caterpillar is 10 m above the ground, calculate:
  a) the time taken to reach the ground.
  b) the vertical velocity with which the caterpillar strikes the ground.
  c) the resultant velocity (both magnitude and direction) with which the caterpillar strikes the ground.

d) the horizontal distance travelled by the caterpillar.

3 Calculate the kinetic energy of the caterpillar as it strikes the ground after falling as in Question 2.

4 Estimate the force with which the caterpillar strikes the ground when it falls as in Question 2.

5 Smaller raindrops of mass 0.5 mg fall vertically with a uniform velocity of 3 m s⁻¹.
  a) Why do they fall at a uniform velocity?
  b) If a horizontal wind is blowing at a uniform velocity of 4 m s⁻¹, calculate the resultant velocity (both magnitude and direction) of the raindrops.

4 ▶ SAFE DRIVING

Look at the table of statistics about car stopping distances and then answer the following questions.

mph	Thinking distance		Braking distance		Overall stopping distance	
	m	ft	m	ft	m	ft
20	6	20	6	20	12	40
30	9	30	14	45	23	75
40	12	40	24	80	36	120
50	15	50	38	125	53	175
60	18	60	55	180	73	240
70	21	70	75	245	96	315

Table 4.1 Shortest stopping distance
On a dry road, a good car with good brakes and tyres and an alert driver will stop in the distances shown. Remember these are shortest stopping distances. Stopping distances increase greatly with wet and slippery roads, poor brakes and tyres, and tired drivers.

FACT FILE

Impulse = change in momentum or
$F \times t = mv - mu$.

Kinetic energy = $\frac{1}{2}mv^2$

Potential energy = mgh

$v = u + at$

$v^2 = u^2 + 2as$

$s = ut + \frac{1}{2}at^2$

$F = ma$
1 mile = 1600 m.

1 a) Why are stopping distances increased in the adverse conditions listed?
b) Why do you think the driver's consumption of alcohol affects stopping distances?

2 Using the table of data, calculate:
a) the initial speeds of the car in m s^{-1}
b) the deceleration during braking for each car speed.

3 A car collides with a wall and is brought to a halt in 0.2 s. If the initial speed of the car is 60 mph and the mass of the car and occupants is 1000 kg, calculate the average force on the car during the collision.

4 How might the average force calculated above be absorbed by the car with least damage to the occupants?

5 The driver of the car in Question 3, who is wearing a safety belt, moves a distance of 0.15 m relative to the car during the crash. The mass of the driver is 80 kg.
a) By considering energy, find out the average force exerted on the driver by the safety belt.
b) How might this force be reduced?

6 Find out what safety features are being introduced:
a) to cars by different car manufacturers.
b) to current driving regulations.

Read the following two newspaper articles carefully and then answer the questions which follow.

JUBILATION IN JUBAKALAND

Last night after more than four hours, during which time he jumped just four times, Sergey Bubka of the Soviet Union became world pole vault champion yet again. He was winner at both previous World Championships and at the 1988 Olympics. He was probably the hottest favourite of the week; even his rivals said they had no chance. But with the bar set at 5.95 m - well over the height of a double-decker bus - Bubka faced a moment of crisis. The 22-year-old Hungarian, Istvan Bagyula, winner at the World Student Games, was already over at 5.90. Bubka had failed once at that level and, having opted not to have another jump in that round, failed again at 5.95. So this was his final chance. It looked tense enough from the stands. But what Bubka knew, and no one else did, was that he was in agony from an injured heel on which he had already had two pain-killing injections. He ran forward, shifted the pole into the jousting position, gathered speed, took off and indeed flew over the bar, probably clearing it by about a foot.

Bagyula had no chance at 5.95 m. Bubka stuck his injured foot in an icebag and declined to raise the bar to have a crack at the record, which he raised to 6.10 m in Malmo earlier this month - a significant figure because it broke what pre-metric athletes would have called the 20-foot barrier had they ever contemplated the possibility of man even approaching such a thing. No one else has yet got close.

Bubka's dominance bewilders even his opponents: the explanation (if I correctly interpret the American Tim Bright, who came sixth) appears to be that he can work up a faster take-off speed than anyone else, which enables him to use a more rigid pole which gives him more lift.

Adapted from an article by Michael Engel, *Guardian*, August 30th 1991

FIVE CENTIMETRES THAT BROKE
A 23-YEAR RECORD

New long jump word record of 8.95 metres is as long as two Ford Sierras nose to tail.

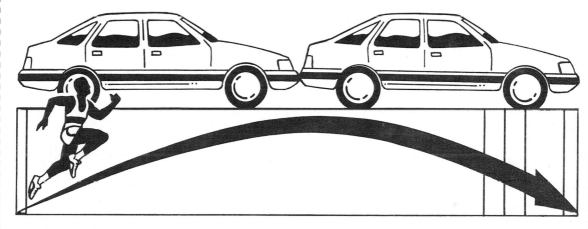

LANDMARKS IN LONG JUMP WORLD RECORDS:

5 Aug 1901 Peter O'Connor (GB) 7.61 metres (24ft 11.5ins)

13 Jun 1925 William Hubbard (US) 7.89 metres (25ft 10.5ins)

25 May 1935 Jesse Owens (US) 8.13 metres (26ft 8.0ins)

18 Oct 1968 Bob Beamon (US) 8.90 metres (29ft 2.5ins)

30 Aug 1991 Mike Powell (US) 8.95 metres (29ft 4.5ins)

The most celebrated mark in athletics was sensationally improved during the World Championships in Tokyo yesterday when Mike Powell, a 27-year-old Philadelphian, leapt 8.95 metres in the long jump. The record had stood at 8.90m (25ft 2.5in) for 22 years and 317 days since Bob Beamon, another American, set it in the high altitude of Mexico City at the 1968 Olympic Games. For the past decade it had withstood the constant assault of Carl Lewis, the outstanding athlete of his generation, who was competing with Powell after establishing a world record for the 100m six days earlier. Unbeaten in the event outdoors since 1980, Lewis was considered to be the man most likely to surpass Beamon and did so with a jump in the fourth round of 8.91m. Lewis was denied the record because of a following wind which exceeded the arbitrary limit of 2 m a second, imposed by the International Amateur Athletic Federation. Lewis's five legal jumps were the greatest series in a single competition, all of them better than Powell's second best. But, as in 1968, the spoils went to a single spectacular effort. Beamon's record was greatly aided by the thin air of high altitude. It was calculated then that without the lesser air resistance at a height of 2.248 m above sea level and the following wind, which was exactly on the legal limit, Beamon's jump would have been only 8.56 m.

Adapted from an article by Michael White, *Guardian*, 20th September 1985

FACT FILE

Kinetic energy = $\frac{1}{2}mv^2$

The following questions relate to the article on page 6.

1 Draw a series of diagrams to illustrate what is happening during a pole vault.
(Hint: divide the pole vault into five stages, i.e. run up, going up, top of the vault, coming down, and landing.)

2 Describe the energy changes that are occuring during each stage of the pole vault. (Use the five stages suggested in Question 1.)

3 a) Draw a graph to illustrate how the pole vaulter's potential energy changes with time during the pole vault. Mark on the position of the pole vaulter at significant points.
b) On the same graph show how the pole vaulter's kinetic energy changes with time.

4 a) Estimate the maximum potential energy that the pole vaulter gains during the world record vault.
b) Do you think his maximum kinetic energy would be greater or less than this?
c) Where does the extra energy go and why can't the energy just disappear?

5 In the article the comment is made that the champion pole vaulter achieves a much faster take–off speed than his rivals and this means that he can use a much stiffer pole.
a) How does the faster take–off speed help?
b) Why do you think using a stiffer pole is an advantage?

The following questions relate to the article on page 7.

6 During the long jump event, several jumps were counted towards the championship but would not have been counted for a world record. The problem was a following wind speed of more than 2 m s^{-1}. During Powell's world record jump the following wind speed was only 0.3 m s^{-1}. Long jump athletes are often compared to world class 100 m runners where the time of such sprint races is around 10 s.
a) estimate the maximum possible differ ence that it would have made to the world record jump by Powell if a wind speed of 2 m s^{-1} had been acting at the time of his jump.
b) What approximations have you made and why is the situation probably much more complex?

7 In the article about the long jump, reference is made to the advantages that Beaman had in 1968. Discuss the reasons for the importance of these advantages.

6 SKY DIVING

At 10,000 feet these skydivers have a terminal velocity of about 125 mph. At 3000 feet the terminal velocity is lower at about 100 mph. These skydivers informed us that they don't notice the difference between these speeds as they were still falling to Earth rather fast! However, this increase in terminal velocity reduces the effectiveness of jumping from the aircraft at a higher altitude in order to increase the time available for freefall. As one of the skydivers remarked - it is effectively a law of diminishing returns.
Other problems encountered by the skydivers are concerned with the difficulty of setting up a group in freefall as in the photograph. One diver trying to join the others can easily cause the group to fly apart and so spoil the pattern.

FACT FILE

Viscous forces opposing motion act on any body moving through a fluid. The viscous force on a sphere falling through a fluid is $6\pi r\eta v$ where r = radius of the sphere, η = viscosity of the fluid, and v = velocity of the sphere.

Archimedes Principle states that any object in a fluid experiences an upthrust from the fluid equal to the weight of fluid displaced.

1 mile = 1600 m

Volume of a sphere = $\frac{4}{3}\pi r^3$

1 What is the downward force on a skydiver?

2 Estimate the total upward force on a skydiver when moving at terminal velocity.

3 a) What forces are acting on a skydiver in freefall?
b) Write down an equation connecting these forces when the skydiver is moving at terminal velocity.

4 Why is the terminal velocity greater at higher altitudes?

5 By considering one skydiver trying to approach another discuss why it is difficult for them to join up.
(Hint: consider a horizontal approach relative to the skydivers in the ring.)

6 a) Assume the mass of the skydiver is 80 kg and the density of air is 1.1 kg m^{-3} at 3000 ft. Calculate an approximate value for the viscosity of air at that height.
b) The value that you have calculated will be of the order of 105 times greater than the value for air at that height. What does that tell you about the validity of any approximations that you have made. What other factors may be acting?

7 a) What will the forces be on the skydiver when he/she eventually opens the parachute?
b) How will the vertical speed of fall of the skydiver change with time after leaving the aeroplane until landing on the ground?

Read the short extract below and then answer the questions which follow.

The Bishop Rock lighthouse near the Isles of Scilly has a helicopter landing pad on the top of it. Using this pad helicopters can land to bring relief crews to the lighthouse. If it is supplies only that are being brought by the helicopter, they are carried in a bag slung below the helicopter. The helicopter then hovers above the landing pad until the load touches the pad. The load is then released by the lighthouse keeper. Around the centre of the landing pad nets are slung between struts. These act as a useful safety net if the load just misses the main landing pad. They are also much appreciated by the lighthouse keeper for sunbathing on a still, warm day.

FACT FILE

The rate of change of momentum of a body is proportional to the external force acting on the body, i.e. $F = \dfrac{d}{dt}(mv)$

When a body is moving in a circle $F = \dfrac{mv^2}{r}$

where F = centripetal force acting on the body towards the centre of the circular path, m = mass of the body and r = radius of the circular path.

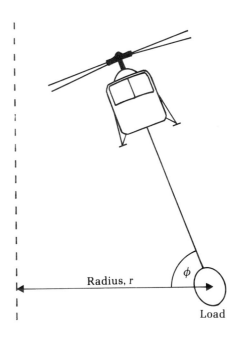

Radius, r

Load

Fig. 7.1

1 The helicopter has a mass of 1500 kg and when it hovers above the lighthouse it does this by giving a downward velocity to the 'cylinder' of air below it. Assume the radius of this cylinder of air is effectively 3 m and the density of air is 1.2 kg m^{-3}.

a) Calculate the lift force needed by the helicopter to remain hovering.

b) State, with reasons, the force that must be exerted on the air below the hovering helicopter.

c) Calculate the downward velocity given to the air by the hovering helicopter.

2 When the helicopter is carrying a load slung underneath it, the load swings out as the helicopter banks round the lighthouse, before hovering and landing. Discuss why the load swings out.

3 If the helicopter is moving round the lighthouse so that a load of 100 kg travels on a circular path of radius 15 m and the speed of the helicopter load is 15 km h^{-1}, calculate:

a) the centripetal acceleration of the load.

b) the centripetal force on the load.

4 By vertical and horizontal resolution of the forces on the load, calculate:

a) the angle ϕ that the cable hooked to the load makes with the horizontal as the helicopter banks round as in Question 3.

b) the tension in the cable supporting the load.

5 A lighthouse keeper sunbathing on a net depresses the centre of the net by 20 cm.

a) Estimate the angle to the horizontal that the net makes at the struts supporting it.

b) Estimate the tension in the net supporting his weight.

6 A helicopter is attempting to fly due North. The speed of the helicopter in still air is 30 km h^{-1}. If there is an easterly cross wind of 20 km h^{-1}, calculate:

a) the direction in which the pilot will need to head the helicopter in order to follow a due North path.

b) the magnitude of the resultant speed of the helicopter relative to the ground.

7 On another day, the helicopter travels about 10 km from St. Mary's to the Bishop Rock lighthouse. If the same helicopter has a following wind on the outward journey of 5 km h^{-1}

calculate:

a) the time needed for the outward journey.

b) the time needed for the return journey.

Read the extract below from a washing machine manual and then answer the questions which follow.

WATER EXTRACTION

Water is removed from clothes by centrifugal force when the drum is rotated at high speed. Clothes are pressed against the sides of the container and water escapes through slots and/or holes in it. A safety device in the door or lid prevents access to the container during spinning.

The amount of water removed depends on the speed of spinning and the diameter of the container. This speed is measured in revolutions per minute (rpm) and varies in different models from 400 to 1200 rpm.

Synthetic fabrics do not absorb as much water as natural ones. If synthetics are spun for too long or spun when hot, creasing of the fabric can result. With the introduction of electronic controls some machines give a selection of spinning speeds to suit different fabrics. Some non-electronic machines vary the time of spinning according to the programme chosen for the type of fabric.

A machine with a low spin speed obviously will not extract as much water from natural fabrics as one with a higher spin speed. It is not possible to extract any more water at a low spin speed after the recommended spinning time is up, so it is a waste of time to give clothes further spinning. After water extraction many fabrics require further drying.

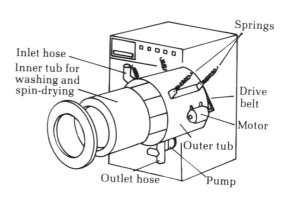

Figure 8.1

Progress display

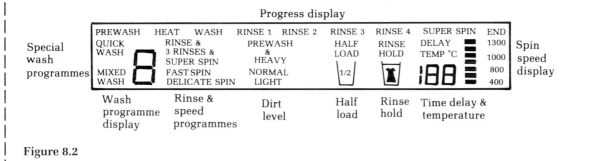

| Special wash programmes | Wash programme display | Rinse & speed programmes | Dirt level | Half load | Rinse hold | Time delay & temperature | Spin speed display |

Figure 8.2

FACT FILE

When a body is moving in a circle $F = mr\omega^2$ where F = centripetal force acting on the body towards the centre of the circular path, m = mass of the body, r = radius of the circular path and ω = the angular speed.

The time period of oscillation of a spring is

$$T = 2\pi\sqrt{\frac{m}{k}}$$

where m = the mass in kg hanging on the spring and k = the spring constant in N m^{-1}.

1 The diagram of an automatic washing machine (see Fig.8.1) shows the outer drum attached to the casing by a number of springs. Discuss what you consider to be the reason for including the springs in the design.

2 Some washing machines have a large block of concrete attached to the outer drum. What do you consider might be the reason for including this in the design?

3 The display panel illustrated in Fig.8.2 shows how rapidly the drum is rotating, in revolutions per minute, during the spin cycle (see *Spin speed display*). The same machine also has a 'natural frequency' of oscillation occuring when the drum rotates at 50 rpm as

the spin speed builds up.
 a) Calculate the frequency of rotation in hertz for each spin speed.
 b) What is meant by *natural frequency* and how will this affect the operation of the machine?

4 The maximum mass of clothes, water and drum can be as much as 20 kg. This gives an approximate maximum loading for each spring of 5 kg. A manufacturer has access to three types of spring with spring constants of 137 N m^{-1}, 556 N m^{-1}, and 1000 N m^{-1} respectively. Which spring should not be chosen for the machine?

5 Explain how water is extracted from the clothes by the spin dryer. (Hint: the statement from the washing machine manual, "Water is removed from clothes by centrifugal force ..." is incorrect.)

6 Estimate the centripetal force on a 500g towel at each of the spin speeds.

7 a) Why do you think that it is not possible to extract any more water at a low spin speed after the recommended spinning time is up?
 b) How might you get more water out of the clothes?
 c) Why do you think cotton materials retain more water than synthetic materials after the same spin programme?

9   ANTIQUE CLOCKS

A Viennese wall clock made in the period from 1850 to 1900 can be spring driven or pendulum and weight driven. The pendulum makes 40 complete swings every minute; this leads to the clock ticking 80 times a minute. In contrast, the grandfather longcase clock ticks once every second.

*F*ACT FILE

The time period of oscillation of a pendulum

is $T = 2\pi \sqrt{\dfrac{l}{g}}$

where l = the length of the pendulum in m and g = the acceleration due to gravity in m s^{-2}

1 **a)** Assuming that the pendulum behaves like a simple pendulum find out an approximate value for the length of the pendulum:
    i) for a Viennese wall clock.
    ii) for a grandfather longcase clock.
b) Why do you think the wall clock became more popular than the longcase clock?
c) Why are the values that you have calculated in a) only approximate?

2 **a)** During a complete swing, when does the pendulum bob have the maximum potential energy?
b) When does the pendulum bob have maximum kinetic energy?
c) When is the kinetic energy of the pendulum bob zero?

3 **a)** Derive an expression for the maximum kinetic energy of the pendulum bob in terms of its mass m, angular frequency w, and amplitude of oscillation a.
(Hint: assume that the bob is undergoing simple harmonic motion.)
b) Why is the above assumption an approximation?
c) If the pendulum bob of the wall clock has a mass of 2 kg and an amplitude of oscillation of 3 cm, calculate the maximum kinetic energy of the bob.

WAVE MOTION

10 ▶ POLARISED WAVES - PROBLEM OR HELP?

Read the following article and then answer the
questions which follow.

Polarised light improves design

Polarised light is being used in industry to establish the
main points of stress in manufactured items. Either the
actual item is coated with photostress plastic or scale
models of the item are made in the same plastic. When
the items are subjected to stress and viewed in a
polariscope, coloured fringes are seen which indicate the
main points of stress and possible areas of weakness in
the design. Our science correspondent understands that
this technique has been used by aeroengineering firms to
establish possible weaknesses in turbine blades. Engi-
neers look at models that have been subjected to scaled
down stresses by running them on test beds.

*F*ACT FILE

Any electromagnetic wave consists of an
electric field component and a magnetic field
component at right angles to each other and to
the direction of propagation.
Unpolarised visible light consists of oscillations of the electric field in all directions
perpendicular to the direction of transmission
of the wave.

Plane polarised light is light where the oscil-
lating electric field is in one direction only.
A polariscope is made of crossed polaroids.
A polaroid only allows through light
with the electric vector vibrating in a
certain plane.

1 **a)** How does the pattern of stress fringes indicate the main points of stress?
b) Explain why the headline in the newspaper article is justified in claiming polarised light improves design.

2 **a)** Find out and discuss why polaroid sunglasses work.
b) A car windscreen is not placed between crossed polaroids so why do you think that fringes are seen when polaroid spectacles are worn in a car?

3 **a)** Explain why you see nothing when viewing a lamp through two pieces of crossed polaroid.
b) In a polariscope the two pieces of polaroid are called the polariser and the analyser. The analyser is nearer your eye. What will you see as the analyser is rotated through 360°?

c) Discuss why you think coloured fringes are seen when using the polariscope.

4 The Science Museum in London has what looks like a stained glass window when viewed through crossed polaroids in white light. It is just transparent, however, when viewed without the polaroids. How do you think this might be done?

5 A liquid crystal display uses crossed polaroids. See if you can find out how one works.

6 Certain liquids such as sugar solution can rotate the plane of polarised light according to the strength of solution.
a) How could you use crossed polaroids to find the angle of rotation?
b) Why might this be useful?

11 ▶ SEISMIC WAVES

Read the article below and then answer the questions which follow.

MEXICO HIT BY EARTHQUAKES

Up to 1,000 people were feared dead last night and hundreds more injured in the rubble of fallen buildings in Mexico City after an earthquake engulfed three Mexican states and shook buildings as far away as Texas.

In sparsely-populated coastal states, a church collapsed during a mass killing 25 people, and ancient cathedrals were also reportedly destroyed. The brunt of the earthquake, measuring 7.8 on the Richter scale, was borne by the Mexican capital, a vast congested city of 18 million people, caught during the morning rush hour.

Mexican embassy officials in Washington identified the central areas of Colonia Roma and Colonia Doctores as the most seriously damaged parts of the city. Television pictures showed a severely damaged hotel near the central Monument of the Revolution. Ham radio operators reported people seeing many dead in the streets and doctors had taken patients "out into the street because they thought it was safer".

The epicentre of the earthquake was thought to be about 40 miles offshore in the Pacific Ocean, 150 miles north-west of Acapulco.

In March, another earthquake registering 7.8 on the Richter scale killed 177 people in Chile, a part of the perpetual movement along the great Pacific fault line which destroyed San Francisco in 1906.

FACT FILE

In refraction of waves $\dfrac{\sin i}{\sin r} = \dfrac{v_1}{v_2}$

where i = the angle of incidence, r = the angle of refraction, v_1 = the velocity in first medium, v_2 = the velocity in second medium.

For S waves, the velocity $v_s = \sqrt{\dfrac{\mu}{\rho}}$

where μ = the rigidity modulus of the medium and ρ = the density.

For P waves, the velocity $v_p = \sqrt{\dfrac{\psi}{\rho}}$

where ψ = the axial modulus of the medium and ρ = the density.

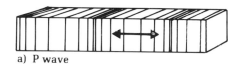

Figure 11.1 S and P waves in rock

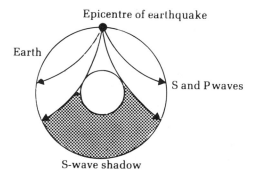

Figure 11.2 Waves from an earthquake

1 From the diagrams in Fig.11.1 on seismic waves passing through rocks, which waves are longitudinal and which are transverse?

2 a) In the article reference is made to *epicentre* and *Richter scale*. What do these terms mean?
b) Why did doctors take their patients outside? Why was the damage so extensive?
c) Reference is made to the *great Pacific fault line*. What is the significance of this region and other similar regions of the Earth?

3 Granite has a density of 2.7×10^3 kg m^{-3}, an axial modulus of 8.5×10^{10} Nm^{-2} and a rigidity modulus of 3.0×10^{10} Nm^{-2}. Calculate the velocities of S and P waves in granite. Which waves will arrive at a seismometer first?

4 a) Calculate the angle of refraction of a P wave, which has an angle of incidence of 20° in a rock layer where the P–wave velocity is 6.1 km s^{-1}, when the wave is refracted into another layer where the P–wave velocity is 8.1 km s^{-1}.
b) What would happen in the same situation to a P–wave incident at an angle of 50°? Support your answer by a calculation.

5 Any liquid has a rigidity modulus = 0. What does the S–wave shadow in Fig.11.2 suggest about the nature of the core of the Earth?

6 a) Using the values of the velocities that you calculated in Question 3, find out how far away an earthquake's epicentre is from a measuring station if a time delay of 120 s is observed between the arrival of P and S waves.
b) What assumption have you made in calculating your answer?

7 The paths shown of S and P waves through the Earth are curved indicating successive refractions and total internal reflection at some stage. What does this tell you about the axial modulus for P waves in rock layers closer to the centre of the Earth given that the density of rocks increases towards the centre?

Read the following article and answer the questions which follow.

BLACK HOLE DISCOVERED

Astronomers have recently come up with the most likely black hole candidate yet. It is the X-ray transient known as A0620-00 (*Nature*, 321, 1 May 1986, page 16) X-ray transients are a sort of X-ray binary system, consisting of a faint red star and an attracting compact object (for example, a black hole). They are transient because they only emit X-rays for relatively short periods, which recur over timescales of years.

Astronomers J E McClintock and R A Remillard have been able to determine the radial velocity curve of the red star to the dense object by measuring the periodic Doppler shift of its absorption lines.

The amplitude found was 457 km s⁻¹, very large for a binary with such a short period (only 9 hours). This means that the dense object must be at least 3.2 times as massive as the sun. This is above the maximum possible mass for a neutron star: the object must be a black hole. Or so the theory goes.

It is no use for the sceptical among you arguing that A0620-00 might be a triple, rather than a binary, by the way. This argument does not hold up given the small size of the system implied by the short 8-hour period.

*F*ACT FILE

When a star, emitting light of wavelength λ, moving relative to an observer with speed v the observed change in wavelength $\Delta\lambda$ is given by:

$\Delta\lambda = \dfrac{v\lambda}{c}$ where c = the speed of light.

This effect is called the Doppler effect. (The above equation assumes the velocity v is much less than the speed of light. When v approaches c relativistic effects have to be taken into account.)

The radial velocity referred to in the article is the maximum velocity observed or calculated as the star moves towards us or away and this can be taken to be the speed of the visible red star round the possible black hole.

Stars moving away from the Earth show a red shift.

Stars moving towards the Earth show a blue shift.

A binary system of stars consists of two stars orbiting round a common centre of gravity.

$c = 3 \times 10^8$ m s⁻¹, $c = f\lambda$, $f = 1/T$, $w = 2\pi f$, $v = rw$

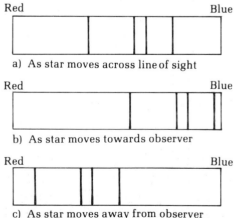

a) As star moves across line of sight

b) As star moves towards observer

c) As star moves away from observer

Figure 12.1

1 Given that stars moving towards the Earth show a blue shift, what would you expect to happen to the wavelength of the X-rays from the X-ray transient red star as it:

    a) moves towards an observer.

    b) moves away from an observer.

2 a) If the X-ray transient star emits X–rays of frequency 10^{19} Hz, calculate the wavelength of the X-rays emitted.

    b) Hence, calculate the change in wavelength as the star moves towards or away from the observer. (Use the maximum amplitude of the radial velocity.)

3 The spectrum of light from a star has characteristic dark lines across it. These are called absorption lines. In the Sun's spectrum they are known as Fraunhofer lines after the scientist who discovered them. Find out and explain how these lines occur and how spectral lines from star spectra give information not only about how the star is moving but also on the elements making up the star.

4 During a total eclipse of the Sun, the dark absorption lines in the Sun's spectrum become bright emission lines. Why does this happen?

5 a) Calculate the frequency of rotation of the star in its orbit.

    b) Hence, calculate the angular velocity of the star.

    c) Now find the radius of orbit of the star.

    d) What is the centripetal acceleration of the star?

6 Astronomers have been hunting black holes for many years but not many have been found. What do you think are the main properties of black holes that make the search difficult?

13 ▶ MUSICAL INSTRUMENTS

Read the Fact file overleaf which accompanies this photograph and then answer the questions which follow.

FACT FILE

For a wave $v = f\lambda$ where v = velocity, f = frequency, and λ = wavelength. In a standing wave the separation between adjacent nodes is $\frac{\lambda}{2}$.

An antinode is found midway between adjacent nodes.

A standing wave in a pipe has an antinode at an open end and a node at a closed end.

A standing wave in a string has a node at each end.

Speed of sound = 340 m s^{-1} at 1 atmosphere and 15°C.

$f_o = \frac{1}{2l}\sqrt{\frac{T}{\mu}}$ where T = tension in the string in N,

μ = the mass/unit length in kg m^{-1} and l = the length of the string in m.

1 **a)** Identify those instruments in the orchestra that have transverse standing waves in them when they are played.
b) Identify those instruments in the orchestra that have longitudinal standing waves in them when they are played.
c) How does the wavelength of the sound waves produced relate to the standing waves in the instruments?
d) How is the volume of sound amplified by the instrument in the case of:
  (i) the violin.   **(iii)** the piano.
  (ii) the drum.   **(iv)** the trombone?

2 **a)** Draw sketches to show how a violin string vibrates. Include the fundamental frequency and the first and second overtones.
b) Derive expressions for the frequency of the note produced in each case in terms of the length of the violin string and the velocity of the transverse wave along the string.

3 **a)** Draw sketches to show how the air in an open pipe vibrates. Include the fundamental frequency and the first and second overtones.
b) Draw sketches to show how the air in a pipe closed at one end vibrates. Include the fundamental frequency and the first and second overtones.
c) Derive expressions for the frequency of the note produced in each case in terms of the length of the pipe and the velocity of the longitudinal wave along the pipe.

4 **a)** Some harmonics are missing from both open pipes and pipes closed at one end. Discuss and explain the reason for this.
b) What does the quality of a note depend on? How will the quality differ between open and closed pipes?

5 **a)** An organ pipe is closed at one end and has a length of 2 m. What is the frequency of the fundamental note emitted?
b) What would be the fundamental frequency emitted if the pipe were open at both ends?
c) If another organ pipe with a length of 2.1 m was sounded at the same time, what would be the frequency of the beats emitted?
d) Would you be able to hear the beats?

6 The fundamental frequency of the notes emitted by the highest strings on the violin, viola and cello are 660 Hz, 440 Hz and 220 Hz respectively.
a) Assuming the velocity of sound is 340 m s^{-1}, calculate the wavelength in each case.
b) If the mass per unit length of the violin string is 0.4 g m^{-1} and the length is 0.3 m, calculate the tension applied to the string to keep it in tune.

7 Describe how the phase and amplitude of the vibrations of different parts of the violin string vary when it is vibrating in:
a) the fundamental mode.
b) the first overtone.

14 REFLECTIVE TOYS AND INSTRUMENTS

Read the article below and then answer the
questions which follow.

To find the angle of elevation of the Sun or a star.

Warning: Do not view the Sun with this instrument
without the glare filters in place - permanent damage
to your eyes may result.

1. Line up the sextant so that the horizon is seen
through the clear glass lower half of the fixed mirror M_1
by looking through the telescope T.

2. Rotate the movable mirror M_2 until the horizon is
also seen, by reflection from M_2 and the silvered upper
half of M_1, coincident with the image viewed directly.
The two mirrors are now parallel. Note the scale
reading giving the position of M_2.

3. Now rotate M_2 until a reflected image of the Sun is
seen through the telescope coincident with the
horizon viewed directly through the lower half of M_1.
Note the new scale reading.

4. The difference between the scale readings gives the
angle rotated by the mirror M_2, which is equal to half
the angle of elevation of the Sun.

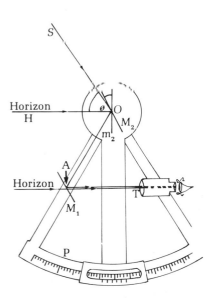

Figure 14.1

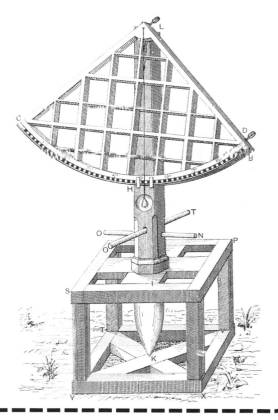

1 A child's kaleidoscope is made with two mirrors inclined at 60° to each other.
a) By drawing to scale, find out how many images are seen by the child using the toy.
b) How will the number of images change if the angle between the mirrors is increased?
c) How will the number of images change if the angle between the images is decreased?
d) Theoretically, how many images will be seen if the mirrors are parallel? Why don't we see quite as many as this?

2 The child's periscope contains two parallel mirrors each inclined at 45° to the vertical.
a) Sketch a ray diagram to find out if the final image is erect or inverted.
b) How might the periscope be adapted to look behind a person?
c) Which way up is the final image now?

3 a) If a single plane mirror is rotated through an angle of 30°, what happens to the position of a ray of light reflected at the mirror? Give reasons.
(Hint: consider a ray of light initially incident along the normal to the mirror.)
b) Study carefully the account of how to use a sextant. Show that the angle rotated by the mirror M_2 is equal to half the angle of elevation of the Sun.
(Hint: consider light going through the sextant in reverse!)

4 A rear view periscope on a car is sometimes used when towing a caravan.
a) Which way up must the final image be?
b) Mirrors are not used, just prisms which give a better, clearer, final image. Why is this?
c) Draw a ray diagram to show how such a periscope might be made using three prisms 45°,45° and 90° respectively, i.e. two to make the periscope and one to be used as an image inverter.
d) Calculate the angles associated with the path of the rays through the inverter prism.

5 A convex rear view mirror is often used in cars instead of a plane mirror. Why is this?

6 Diamonds are cut to give a maximum brilliant effect. What will be happen to light striking a cut diamond?

7 A girl of height 1.7 m stands in front of a mirror. What is the shortest mirror that will let her see her full reflection and where must it be placed on the wall?
(Hint: draw a ray diagram.)

15 ULTRASOUND IMAGING

Read the article below and then answer
the questions which follow.

——— USING ULTRASOUND IN MEDICINE ———

Ultrasonic waves are sound waves with frequencies which are too high to be detected by the human ear. When ultrasonic waves of frequencies in the range 1 to 3 MHz are transmitted into the human body a picture of the structure of the tissue and bone within the body can be built up from the partial reflections that occur at tissue boundaries. This is done by analysing the time lapse between the outgoing signal and the returning signal and monitoring the signal's intensity. This technique is useful as it causes no damage to the body.

Reflections occur because there is a difference in the acoustic impedance Z of each substance. There is no reflection when the acoustic impedance of two materials is the same.

An ultrasonic transducer is used which can generate and detect ultrasonic waves. Acoustic matching is important between the transducer probe and the skin. This ensures no reflections from outside the body and is achieved with a gel or oil. The transducer probe also contains position sensors. These send signals to the X and Y plates of a cathode ray oscilloscope which place the spot from the electron gun. The brightness of the spot is controlled by the intensity of the received reflected signal. A picture is then built up as the probe is moved over the area examined.

This technique is now used to scan the baby whilst in the womb and is particularly useful for checking the baby's growth and ascertaining the position of the baby before birth.

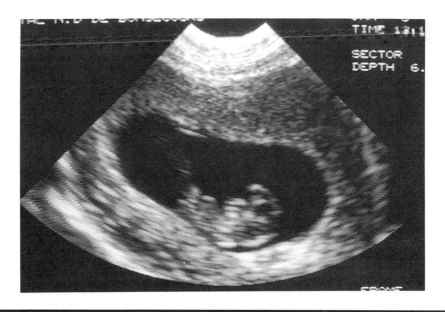

FACT FILE

Acoustic impedance $Z = rv$ kg m^{-2} s^{-1} where
r = the density of the material and
v = the ultrasound velocity in the material.
For reflection at a boundary between two
materials the intensity reflection coefficient a
is:

$\dfrac{I_r}{I_i} = \dfrac{(Z_2 - Z_1)^2}{(Z_2 + Z_1)^2}$ where I_r = the reflected intensity,

I_i = the incident intensity,
Z_1 = the acoustic impedance of the medium
containing the incident ultrasound and
Z_2 = the acoustic impedance of the medium
on the other side of the boundary.
$v = f\lambda$

1 For an ultrasound wave of frequency 2 MHz,
calculate the wavelength in:
    a) bone, where v = 4080 m s^{-1}.
    b) soft tissue, where v = 1500 m s^{-1}

2 The density of air is 1.3 kg m^{-3}, of soft tissue
is 1060 kg m^{-3}, and of bone is on average
1700 kg m^{-3}.
    a) Given that the ultrasound velocity in air
    is 330 m s^{-1}, calculate the acoustic imped-
    ance for all three materials.

b) By consideration of the magnitude of the
intensity reflection coefficient, decide what
will happen when ultrasound is directed at
boundaries between these materials.

3 Using the laws of refraction, investigate
what happens when a beam of ultrasound is
incident at an angle of incidence of 30° at a
boundary between fat (ultrasound
velocity = 1450 m s^{-1}) and muscle (ultrasound
velocity = 1590 m s^{-1}).

4 Ultrasound passing from a liquid to a solid
generally increases in velocity. What shape
should a converging lens for ultrasound be in
this case? Support your argument with a ray
diagram.

5 Describe how a picture of the body is built
up from ultrasound. What do you think might
be the limitations of this technique?

6 By focusing and increasing the power,
ultrasound has been used to break up gall
stones in patients. What precautions would
you think might have to be observed with this
technique?

7 Ultrasound is also used for sonar ranging by
fishing fleets. In seawater, the velocity of
ultrasound is 1530 m s^{-1}. If an echo is detected
from a shoal of fish, the time delay is 25 ms,
what is the depth of the shoal?

16 RAINBOWS

Read the article below and then answer the
questions which follow.

Since early times we have marvelled at the miracle
of a rainbow hanging in the sky. While legends of
crocks of gold and other myths have encouraged
people to try to find the end of the rainbow, throughout the ages scientists have tried to work out how
this beautiful phenomenon occurs.

In ancient Greece, Aristotle decided a rainbow was
due to unusual reflections of sunlight from clouds.
In the thirteenth century, Roger Bacon measured the
angle between the rainbow rays and the incident
sunlight. He found this was 42° for the primary bow
and 50° for the secondary bow. In the fourteenth
century, Theodoric, a German monk, suggested a
rainbow was formed by each drop in a cloud and

experimented with a ray of light
passing through a flask. The famous mathematician and scientist
Descartes, not knowing about
Theodoric's work, did the same
experiment in the seventeenth century. They both found that a single
internal reflection was involved in
the primary rainbow and that two
internal reflections were involved
in the secondary rainbow.

The laws of refraction were discovered by Snell in 1621 and these
helped explain the internal reflections observed. The colours of the
rainbow were finally explained by
Newton when he performed his prism experiments in
1666 and demonstrated the dispersion of sunlight.
Because of the variations of the refractive index of
water for the different colours of light, Newton was
able to show that the rainbow angle (the angle of
deflection of the incident sunlight e.g. 180° – 42° for
a primary bow) varied from 137° 58′ for red light to
139° 43′ for violet light. Complicated wave me-
chanic mathematical treatments and consideration
of the behaviour of photons has led to a more detailed
picture of the theory of the rainbow being built up by
scientists in this century, giving more accurate results.

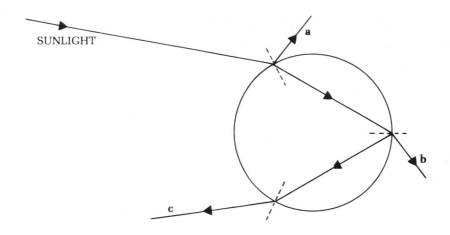

SUNLIGHT

Figure 16.1 How a primary rainbow is formed

Fact File

In refraction $\dfrac{\sin i}{\sin r}$ = refractive index where i = the angle of incidence and r = the angle of refraction.
Mean refractive index for water = 1.33

1 **a)** Why does the internal reflection mentioned in the article happen?
   b) What is the mean critical angle for water?

2 Using the information given in the article, what is the angular width or dispersion of the colours of a primary rainbow?

3 Discuss and explain why a rainbow makes an arc in the sky.

4 The diagram in Fig.16.1 shows three ways a ray can be reflected and refracted by a drop of water.
   a) Describe what is happening in each case.
   b) Which ways will give rise to a spectrum?

5 Redraw the diagram and show the paths of red and violet rays through the drop for the primary rainbow.
(Hint: consider which will be refracted the most by the drop.)

6 **a)** Where else can you see rainbow colours?
   b) Are these colours always due to dispersion? What other mechanism can be involved?

7 In his experiments with sunlight, suppose Newton used a 60° prism of glass with refractive index of 1.510 for red light and 1.521 for blue light and an angle of incidence at the first face of the prism of 30°.
   a) Calculate the dispersion that occurs at the first face of the prism.
   b) Calculate the total angular deviation of the red light after it has passed through the prism.
   c) Calculate the total angular deviation of the blue light after it has passed through the prism.
   d) Calculate the angular dispersion of the final spectrum produced.

17 ▸ FIBRE OPTICS IN MEDICINE

Read the article below and then answer the following questions.

LOOKING INSIDE THE BODY

Light can be carried to inaccessible places in the body using a fibre optic endoscope. This consists of a flexible tube containing bundles of glass fibres which allow light to travel along them. Light can travel down a bundle of fibres from a source into the body and then another bundle of fibres with lenses is used to transmit an image back to the eyepiece. The image is seen because each fibre transmits a tiny part of the whole image and the fibres are always in exactly the same position in the tube relative to each other. This is known as a coherent bundle. An incoherent bundle can be used for just the transmission of light.

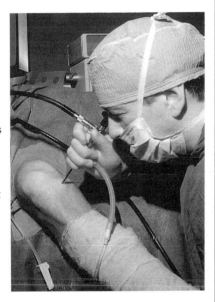

Each fibre is surrounded by cladding of a lower refractive index. Light then travels down the fibre as long as the angle of incidence at the core/cladding interface is greater than or equal to the critical angle. Repeated total internal reflections occur as the light travels down the fibre.

A fibre optic endoscope can be used to look at the colon, the gastrointestinal tract, the pancreas and many other organs of the body.

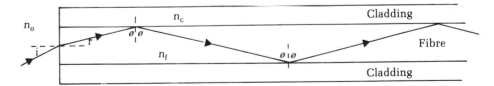

Figure 17.1 Light travelling down a glass fibre

$$\frac{\sin i}{\sin r} = \frac{n_f}{n_o} \text{ and } \sin \phi_c = \frac{n_c}{n_f}$$

where i = angle of incidence outside the fibre, r = angle of refraction of light in the fibre, n_o = refractive index of the material outside the fibre, n_f = refractive index of fibre, n_c = refractive index of the cladding, ϕ_c = critical angle.
If $\phi \geq \phi_c$ then total internal reflection occurs, where ϕ = the angle of incidence at the fibre/cladding interface.

1 What do you think are the main advantages in medicine of using a fibre optic endoscope?

2 a) What happens to the light in the fibre when it is incident on the fibre/cladding interface at an angle less than the critical angle ϕ_c?
b) When might this happen when using the fibre optic endoscope in the body? Support your answer with a diagram.

3 Using the equations given in the fact file and the diagram in Fig.17.1, show that

$$n_o \sin i = n_f \sqrt{1 - \sin^2 \phi} \,.$$

4 $i = i_{max}$ when the angle of incidence is at the largest value possible for total internal reflection to occur, i.e. $\phi = \phi_c$. Using the equation in Question 3, show that

$$n_o \sin i_{max} = \sqrt{n_f^2 - n_c^2} \,.$$

5 $n_o \sin i_{max}$ is called the numerical aperture of the fibre and i_{max} is called the half angle of the fibre as it is half of the maximum field of view that can be transmitted.
   a) Calculate the numerical aperture and the half angle of a fibre in air when the fibre has a refractive index of 1.58 and a cladding of refractive index 1.45.
   b) How do the numerical aperture and the half angle change when the fibre is used in water? (Refractive index = 1.33.)

6 a) Describe the essential differences between a coherent bundle of light fibres and a non–coherent bundle.
   b) How will the diameter of each individual fibre affect the quality of the image?

7 Optics fibres cannot transmit light indefinitely as there is a loss of intensity as light travels down the fibre. Suggest possible reasons for this.

18 THE HUBBLE TELESCOPE

Read the two articles below and overleaf and then answer the questions which follow.

THE TESTING ERROR THAT LED TO HUBBLE MIRROR FIASCO

NASA has established how a mirror aboard its $1.5 billion Hubble Telescope came to be the wrong shape. The agency said last week that errors in a test instrument apparently led Perkin-Elmer, which fabricated the optics, to finish the 2.4-metre primary mirror of the Hubble Space Telescope incorrectly. Tests by NASA earlier this month showed that a lens in the test instrument, called the "reflective null corrector", is about a millimetre askew. Preliminary analysis indicates that an error of this magnitude could cause the spherical aberration that prevents Hubble from focusing sharply.

The crucial error, the misalignment of a lens by a millimetre, is "very large" by optical standards, says Daniel Schroeder, an astronomer at Beloit College in Wisconsin, and a codesigner of Hubble. In some optical instruments, positions are measured to a fraction of the wavelength of light, less than 1 thousandth of a millimetre.

Perkin-Elmer, which built Hubble at its Danbury plant in Connecticut, tested the primary and secondary mirrors separately, but no one tested the complete telescope before launch. An earlier check by NASA absolved the design itself of blame, leading the agency to narrow the inquiry to possible errors in the testing of the mirrors. The reflective null corrector is a cylinder 76 centimetres high and about half a metre wide. It contains two mirrors and a lens, made specifically to test the Hubble primary. By passing light between two mirrors and through a field lens, the instrument should have generated a wavefront matching the desired shape of the primary mirror. The mirror was finished to match the wavefront, so errors in the corrector meant that the final mirror had the wrong shape (see diagram).

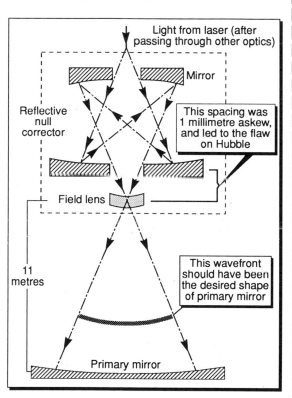

Figure 18.1

DESIGN FLAW CRIPPLES HUBBLE TELESCOPE

Problems with the Hubble Space Telescope pushed questions about NASA's ability to manage big projects into the political spotlight last week. The multi-billion-dollar telescope cannot focus light as well as expected, and the debacle may place a question mark over future funding of large controversial projects, such as the space station.

As *New Scientist* went to press, NASA believed that Hubble's problems could be traced to a design flaw in the primary mirror. The mirror was completed nine years ago, and this month's hearings will look at how it was possible to build a design flaw into the telescope nine years before it was finally launched. That design flaw means that Hubble's observations in the visible part of the spectrum will be little better than is possible from the ground.

Hubble observes in the visible, ultraviolet and infrared parts of the spectrum, and was intended to see objects 10 times smaller than anything recorded to date. In technical terms, it should have a spatial resolution of 0.1 arc seconds compared to the 1 arc second resolution possible with the most ground-based telescopes.

Now, according to Robin Lawrence, the ESA's project scientist for Hubble, the telescope will have a resolution of 0.7 arc seconds. On clear nights, ground-based telescopes can achieve this degree of resolution, and, during the next few years, a new generation of ground-based telescopes will routinely achieve this resolution. Mission controllers moved the telescope's secondary mirror through six positions in an attempt to find the best possible focus. The results they recorded are typical of what is called a spherical aberration (see Diagram). Lawrence says: "If the central part of the mirror is focusing light, the outer part is not, and if the outer part focuses light, the inner part does not."

The effect is that the light is spread out rather than tightly focused. Both ultraviolet and visible observations are equally affected. But ultraviolet observations are not possible from the ground, so Hubble can still do good science at ultraviolet wavelengths.

In the next few months, investigators will determine whether NASA set the wrong specification for one of the mirror to the wrong specification.

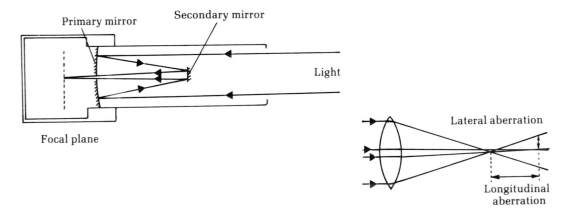

Figure 18.2 No one checked whether Hubble's two mirrors (left) could work together
Inset (right): the principle of aberration.

$\dfrac{1}{u} + \dfrac{1}{v} = \dfrac{1}{f}$ (Real is positive) where

u = object distance from the lens,
v = image distance from the lens.

Magnification = $\dfrac{v}{u}$

1 In the first article what problems were the scientists encountering when they tried to focus the telescope?

2 What possibilities were put forward as reasons for these problems?

3 An object is placed 10.5 cm in front of a converging lens of focal length 10.0 cm.
   a) Calculate the position of the image produced by the lens.
   b) Calculate the new position of the image if the lens is moved 1 mm further away from the object.

c) What is the percentage increase of the object distance?
d) What is the percentage change in the image distance?
e) What is the percentage change in the magnification produced?

4 The second article pinpoints the mistake that was made with the Hubble telescope. Why should an error of only one millimetre have such a big effect on the manufacture of the mirror?

5 Why are mirrors used to gather radiation in the Hubble telescope rather than large lenses?

6 Why is it an advantage to have a telescope in space rather than on the Earth?

7 When using the reflective null corrector, what would happen to the wavefront generated when it exactly matches the shape of the primary mirror?

Read this article and then answer the questions which follow.

HELPING EYESIGHT

The variety of options available at the opticians can prove bewildering. We hope this article will give you some idea of how the different lenses available can help you.

Short-sight (Myopia)

With this condition the image of distant objects appears fuzzy. As Diagram 1 shows the image (I) is formed in front of the retina of the eye. Simple diverging lenses in glasses or hard/soft contact lenses can correct this defect.

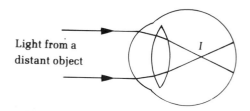

Light from a
distant object

I

Diagram 1 Short sight

Long-sight (Hypermetropia)

With this condition the image of near objects can appear fuzzy. As Diagram 2 shows the image (I) is now formed behind the retina. Simple converging lenses in glasses or hard/soft contact lenses can correct this defect.

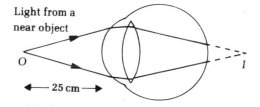

Light from a
near object

O

◄── 25 cm ──►

I

Diagram 2 Long sight and presbyopia

Problems reading when middle-aged (Presbyopia)

When a book has to be held further and further away to be seen in focus help is needed. The problem here is that increased rigidity of the eye lens prevents the lens being pushed to a sufficiently rounded shape by the eye muscles to bring close images into focus on the retina. Again converging lenses are needed to correct this defect.

A combination of problems

Sometimes bifocals or even trifocals are needed to correct for reading, middle distance vision and distance vision. Often varifocal lenses are used where the focal length changes gradually from the lower portion of the lens to the top. However these lenses do not give a very wide field of view which can pose a problem for some users. To obtain a wide field of view D-shaped bifocals or executive bifocals may be more useful. Contact lenses give the best field of view but are not always suitable when there is a combination of problems. Your optician will advise you.

Diagram 3 D-shaped bifocals

Diagram 4 Executive bifocals

FACT FILE

The least distance of distinct vision for the normal eye at which it is comfortable to read is 25 cm.

The power of a lens in dioptres

$$= \frac{1}{\text{Focal length in m}}$$

$$\frac{1}{u} + \frac{1}{v} = \frac{1}{f} \text{ (Real is positive) where}$$

u = object distance from the lens,
v = image distance from the lens.
The focal length of a diverging lens is taken to be negative.
The focal length of a converging lens is taken to be positive.

1 With ray diagrams, show why different types of lenses are needed to correct:
   a) short sight.
   b) long sight.

2 What do you consider are:
   a) the main advantages of contact lenses?
   b) the main disadvantages?

3 Bifocal lenses can cause people to 'miss a step' on a flight of stairs. Why do you think this happens?

4 A middle-aged artist wants to be able to see a whole sheet of A3 paper at once and then view the landscape she is painting.
   a) What type of glasses would you recommend for her?
   b) Why would a pair of varifocal lenses not be suitable?

5 A long–sighted eye has a far point at infinity and a near point at 40 cm. Calculate the power of a suitable correcting lens to allow reading at a comfortable distance from the eye.

6 A short–sighted eye has a far point of 20 cm and a near point of 10 cm.
   a) Calculate the power of a suitable correcting lens for clear distance vision.
   b) Where will a book need to be placed in order for this lens to produce an image at the eye's near point?
   c) Will bifocals be necessary?

7 All spectacle lenses have a concave surface closest to the eye.
   a) How can you tell from the shape of the lens whether it will converge or diverge light?
   b) Why do you think spectacle lenses are made like this? Support your argument with ray diagrams.

F_{ACT} FILE

The amount of light that reaches the film in a camera is proportional to the square of the diameter d of the aperture.

For distant objects the image on the film has an area approximately proportional to the square of the focal length f of the lens.

The amount of light per unit area of image

$$\propto \frac{d^2}{f^2} \text{ and the exposure time} \propto \frac{f^2}{d^2}$$

The ratio $\frac{f}{d}$ is known as the f–number or the relative aperture.

1 If in a camera the f–number is reduced by one setting, find out what happens to the area of the aperture and the exposure time needed?

2 A high f–number setting gives a greater depth of field. Discuss what you think this statement means and give an explanation supported by ray diagrams.

3 A camera is set at aperture $f/5.6$ and forms an image of a distant object on film at a distance of 50 mm from the optical centre of the lens.
  a) What is the focal length of the lens?
  b) What is the effective diameter of the lens?

4 The same camera as in Question 3 needs to be refocussed on an object 0.25 m away. What movement of the optical centre of the lens will be necessary to get a sharp image on the film?

5 A zoom lens has a focal length which can be varied from 30 to 80 mm. The lens is made of several component lenses.
  a) How do you think the overall focal length is altered?
  b) What is the maximum movement of the zoom lens, as a whole, from the film when viewing a distant object?
  c) When using the zoom on an object 3 m away, what is the movement of the whole zoom lens?

6 A camera takes a picture at an exposure time of 1/250 second and an aperture setting of f/4.
  a) If the aperture is changed to f/16, what exposure time is needed to produce the same brightness of image?
  b) What other effect will this change have?

7 Find out as many specialised applications of photography as possible. Which ones use parts of the electromagnetic spectrum outside the visible range?

21 CONCERT HALLS

Amazing strides in Concert Hall design

Concert halls built in Victorian times such as the Albert Hall were designed with little thought about what the audience would be able to see or hear. Indeed, at some points in the Albert Hall most of the orchestra was obscured by pillars while at other points it was possible to hear some notes twice instead of once!

Other problems included areas of the hall where sections of the orchestra were missing from the music heard and other areas where some sections of the orchestra seemed much louder than others. This could have been due to the location of the seating area relative to various sections of the orchestra or interference may have been involved. Nowadays the importance of designing a building to be acoustically correct is appreciated much more. The time taken for a sound to die away to one millionth of its original value is very important. It is called the rever-

beration time. It depends on the absorption and reflection of sounds by the walls, the curtains and the audience and is crucial to the quality of the music heard. If it is too short the sound heard seems lifeless, and if it is too long the sound is too echoing and bathroomish! The reverberation time that is desirable for such buildings can be calculated and the building constructed so that this is achieved. However the desirable reverberation time varies for different sound, e.g. speech, orchestras and choirs. Obviously some compromises have to be made if a multipurpose hall is being designed.

Even places like the Albert Hall can be improved by using modern sound absorbent materials to reduce reflections and changing seating plans to avoid areas with acoustic problems.

FACT FILE

$T = r(0.012 \, V^{1/3} + 0.11)$
where T = the desired reverberation time in s,
V = the volume of the hall in m^3,
and r = a constant which is equal to 4 for speech, 5 for orchestras and 6 for choirs.

1 Explain with a diagram why it might have been possible to hear a note twice in some places in the circular Albert Hall. How might this problem be put right?

2 The position of a listener or interference are given as possible reasons for finding odd silences or amplifications. Explain how this might happen.

3 A concert hall has a volume of 10 000 m^3. Calculate the desired reverberation time for speech, orchestras and choirs.

4 Find out about the ways in which modern sound insulation is used and about the different materials and surfaces that are used in modern buildings to control reverberation.

5 A note of frequency 1.5 kHz is sounded behind a screen made of vertical bars of separation 0.5 m. The note is heard better in some directions than others. Taking the speed of sound as 330 m s^{-1}, calculate these directions. What is the screen acting as?

WAVES, RINGS AND ATOMS

The very nature of crystals is being probed by two powerful techniques. These are X-ray and electron diffraction. By bombarding crystal samples with an X-ray or electron beam, ring patterns are obtained and photographed. These rings are evidence of the atoms that make up the samples. The separation of the rings give vital clues about the arrangement of the atoms or ions in the crystals and indeed give evidence for the very existence of atoms in materials.

This pioneering work was begun in 1914 by Sir William Bragg and his son Lawrence Bragg using X-ray diffraction by reflection from crystal samples. The work was continued by Davisson and Germer who showed that similar diffraction patterns could be obtained by bombarding a thin layer of graphite with a beam of electrons showing that such a beam has wave properties. The wavelength of such a beam depends on the speed of the electrons. The greater the speed the smaller the wavelength. Powerful electron microscopes continue to utilise this technique and can resolve far greater detail than optical microscopes.

Our science correspondent tells us that diffraction patterns can also be observed by looking through umbrella fabric at a sodium street lamp. A small prize is available to the first reader to write in to *Scientific Weekly* describing what is seen and explaining the mechanism for this effect.

Electron diffraction micrograph of silicon showing the atomic arrangement

Read the article above and answer the questions which follow.

*F*ACT FILE

Bragg's equation $2d\sin \varnothing = n\lambda$ where λ = the wavelength of incident X-rays reflecting and diffracting from layers of atoms within the crystal, n = 1,2,3... d = separation of the atomic layers, $\varnothing$ = angle between the incident X-ray beam or the reflected X-ray beam and the reflecting plane.

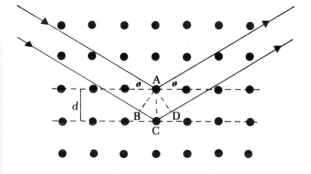

Figure 22.1 Bragg reflections from crystal planes

Diffraction grating equation $d\sin \phi = n\lambda$
where λ = the wavelength of incident beam,
ϕ = diffraction angle to bright maxima,
n = order of diffraction = 1,2,3...
d = grating spacing.

$\lambda = \dfrac{h}{p}$ where λ = wavelength of an electron

with momentum p and
h = Planck constant.

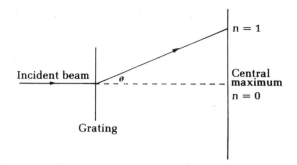

Figure 22.2 Diffraction of a grating

1 a) Describe and justify the diffraction pattern observed when looking through umbrella fabric at a sodium street lamp.
b) Given the wavelength of sodium light is 589 nm, estimate a possible angle from the straight–through direction at which you can see the first bright bit of the pattern as you look out from the centre of the pattern.

2 a) Why are the ring patterns evidence of the atoms that make up the samples?
b) Why do they give vital clues about the arrangement of the atoms or ions in the crystals?
c) Why are diffraction patterns evidence for the wave properties of a beam of electrons?

3 By consideration of path difference, derive the Bragg equation.

4 A crystal of sodium chloride gives a first order diffraction image when an angle of $5.4°$ exists between the incident X-ray beam and the crystal planes. The wavelength of the X-rays is 0.05 nm. Calculate the separation of the atomic planes.

5 a) A beam of electrons is accelerated across a potential difference of 15 kV before striking a target. Calculate the kinetic energy of an electron before striking the target if the electronic charge $e = 1.6 \times 10^{-19}$ C.

b) What is the speed of the electron if the mass of an electron $m = 9.1 \times 10^{-31}$ kg?
c) What is the momentum of the electron?

6 a) What is the wavelength of the electron beam described in Question 5 if $h = 6.6 \times 10^{-34}$ Js?
b) An ordinary diffraction grating has 500 lines per mm. Calculate the first order diffraction angle if such a beam was used.
c) What sized gaps would a diffraction grating have to have in order to get appreciable diffraction effects?

7 If a beam of a particular wavelength passes through a single slit, diffraction occurs given by the equation $d\sin \phi = \lambda$, where d is now the width of the slit and ϕ is the angle to the first position of *minimum* intensity from the normal.
a) Estimate ϕ for a person running through a door.
b) Why don't we observe people diffraction?
c) Why do you think that an electron microscope would have better resolution than an optical microscope?

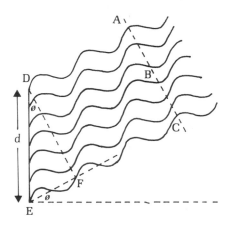

Figure 23.1

1 Why are good quality stands vital for getting maximum performance from a loudspeaker?

2 a) Why does the diagram show the first position of minimum intensity?
b) By using the diagram, derive the equation $d\sin \phi = \lambda$

3 Calculate the angular spread of sound from a loudspeaker of diameter 250 mm if:
a) the frequency of the sound is 1.5 kHz.
b) the frequency of the sound is 10 kHz.
(Take the speed of sound as 330 m s^{-1}.)

4 How does a loudspeaker manufacturer get around the problem highlighted by your answers to Question 3?

5 Discuss why different types of music might be best heard on speakers with different characteristics.

$F_{ACT\ FILE}$

What we hear from an individual loudspeaker depends on the wavelength, λ, of the sound listened to, the angle, ϕ, to the straight ahead direction and the diameter of the speaker d. $d\sin \phi = \lambda$ gives the first position of minimum intensity, as the diagram in Fig.2.31 shows, so an angle of 2ϕ gives the main angular spread of sound.

ELECTRICITY, FIELDS AND ELECTROMAGNETISM

24 A HAND DRYER

The specifications below are those of a hot–air hand dryer used at a heliport in England.

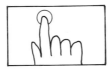

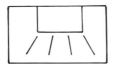

WORLD ® DRYER	*Warner Howard*	**MODEL**	A 48
World Dryer Corporation,	*Exclusive Distributor,*	**SRL**	174107
Berkley, IL, USA	*4 Exmoor St,*	**50 Hz AC**	10A 240 V
	London W10 6DW	**PAT NOS**	2553846

INCLUDING
1A MOTOR

Figure 24.1

FACT FILE

$V - IR$, where V = the potential drop across a conductor in volts, I = the current through the conductor in amps and R = the resistance of the conductor in ohms.

$P = VI$, where P = the power dissipated in watts.

Kirchhoff's Laws (i) $\Sigma I = 0$, i.e. the sum of the currents entering a junction in a circuit is equal to the sum of the currents leaving the junction. (ii) $\Sigma E = \Sigma IR$, i.e. the sum of the e.m.f.s in a circuit is equal to the sum of the potential drops in the circuit.

1 From the data:
   a) what two components make up the dryer circuit?

   b) is the motor in parallel or in series with the heater?

2 The specifications above refer to the entire dryer. What is the current through the heater?

3 What power is used:
   a) by the heater?
   b) by the motor?

4 Estimate the cost of use per week if the dryer is used by ten passengers per flight and there are twelve flights per day excluding Sundays.

5 The voltage quoted is mains a.c.. What is the peak value of this a.c.?

6 When first switched on the heater has more current flowing through it than later. Why?

7 When first switched on the motor has a maximum current flowing through it which decreases to a steady value. Why?

Look at the diagram and table below and then answer the following questions.

Stop/tail light	12V	21W or 5W
Tail light (number plate)	12V	5W
Sidelight	12V	5W
Headlamp	12V	60W or 55W
Reversing light	12V	21W

Table 25.1 Specifications for car lights

*F*ACT FILE

$V = IR$ where V = the potential drop across a conductor in volts, I = the current through the conductor in amps and R = the resistance of the conductor in ohms.
$P = VI$ where P = the power dissipated in watts.
Kirchhoff's Laws i) $\Sigma I = 0$, i.e. the sum of the currents entering a junction in a circuit is equal to the sum of the currents leaving the junction. (ii) $\Sigma E = \Sigma IR$, i.e. the sum of the e.m.f.s in a circuit is equal to the sum of the potential drops in the circuit.
Assume the car battery has negligible internal resistance.

1 a) Using the table of specifications for each type of bulb used in the car lighting circuit, calculate the working current through each.
   b) The initial current through each type of bulb will be greater. Why?

2 Why are all the car lights arranged in parallel (see Fig.25.1)?

3 Calculate the total current drawn from the battery when the car is stationary and:
   a) the side and tail lights are on.

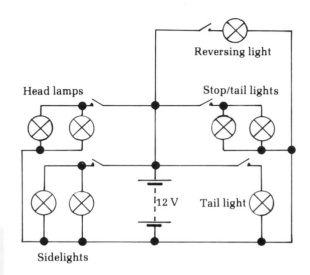

Figure 25.1 Simplified car lighting circuit

   b) the headlights are on full, the reversing light is on and the brakes are on as well.

4 Why is less net current drawn from the battery when the car is in motion?

5 Again using the table of specifications for each bulb:
   a) calculate the working resistance of each bulb.
   b) calculate the eqivalent single resistor that would draw the same amount of current from the battery as in Question 3b).

6 a) Imagine the lights are left on accidentally. When the ignition is switched off, the circuits left on contain the side and tail lights only. How much energy is dissipated if the car is left in this state for ten hours?
   b) The 12 V battery in the car concerned is capable of delivering 1 A for 24 hours before becoming flat. Will the car now start?

7 a) If the car battery was replaced with one with an e.m.f. of 12 V but with an internal resistance of 2 Ω, calculate:

   i) the current in each part of the circuit if only the side and tail lights are operating.

   ii) the voltage across each lamp in this case.

   iii) the new working power of the side and tail bulbs.

b) What would happen to the brightness of the bulbs?

26 POWER TRANSMISSION

FACT FILE

$V = IR$ where V = the potential drop across a conductor, I = the current through the conductor and R = the resistance of the conductor.

$P = VI$ where P = the power dissipated.

$R = \dfrac{\rho l}{A}$ where r = the resistivity of the material, l = the length, and A = the cross–sectional area.

$\dfrac{N_s}{N_p} = \dfrac{V_s}{V_p}$ where N_s = number of turns on a secondary coil, N_p = number of turns on a primary coil, V_s = voltage across the secondary coil and V_p = voltage across the primary coil.

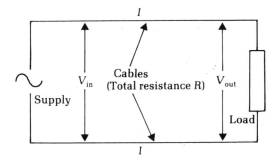

Figure 26.1 Getting power to a load

1 a) Write down the relationship between the power supplied, the power available at the load and the power wasted in the transmission cables.

b) Restate the relationship in terms of the supply voltage V_{in}, the voltage across the load V_{out}, the total resistance of the cables R, and the current in the circuit I.

2 What strategies can be used to make the maximum possible power available at the load?

3 In transmission cables the resistance is kept down by using wires of low resistivity and high cross sectional area.

   a) What may now become a problem with the wires?

   b) How could this be avoided?

4 In the laboratory a 6 V battery with negligible internal resistance is used to supply power to a lamp of resistance 6 Ω. The supply wires have a total resistance of 3 Ω. Calculate:

   a) the current flowing in the circuit.

   b) the power loss in the wires.

   c) the power available at the lamp.

Material	Cross-sectional area/mm²	Resistivity/Ω m	Density /kgm⁻³
Copper	0.1963	1.7×10^{-8}	8 930
Copper	0.007854	1.7×10^{-8}	8 930
Aluminium	0.1963	2.7×10^{-8}	2 700
Aluminium	0.007854	2.7×10^{-8}	2 700
Iron	0.1963	10.5×10^{-8}	7 870
Iron	0.007854	10.5×10^{-8}	7 870

5 Two transmission cables of total length 10 m need to be made so that both the resistance and the weight are as low as possible.

a) Using the data in the table above, calculate the weight and resistance of individual strands of the cables in each case using the data above and select the appropriate wires.

b) Cost will also be a factor in the choice. Find out about relative costings and see if your findings affect your final choice.

6 a) If the 6 V battery in Question 5 is replaced with a 6 V a.c. supply capable of supplying the same power as the battery, design a circuit that will reduce the power loss in the supply wires.
(Safety criterion: you are not allowed to have a voltage drop of greater than 50 V a.c. anywhere in your circuit.)

b) Estimate the new power available using your design.

27 MOSTLY NATURAL SATELLITES

Study the table below carefully and then answer the questions on the opposite page.

Planet	Satellites	Radius of orbit/10⁶m	Period of orbit/days	Radius of satellite/km	Mass of satellite/10²¹ kg
Earth	Moon	384	27.32	1738	73.5
Jupiter	Io	422	1.77	1670	73
	Europa	671	3.55	1460	47.5
	Ganymede	1070	7.15	2550	154
	Callisto	1883	16.69	2360	95
Saturn	Titan	1222	15.95	2440	137
Neptune	Triton	353	5.88	2000	140

Table 29.1 Data on some of the natural satellites in the Solar system (those with radius > 1000km).

The planets in the Solar system have many satellites and recent space journeys such as that made by Voyager have established more rings and satellites than were previously thought to exist. Saturn while remarkable for its spectacular ring system also has one large satellite, Titan, and many smaller satellites. Mars has two tiny satellites, Phobos and Deimos, which have radii of only 6 and 3 km respectively. Jupiter has 12 satellites but the four largest were easily visible to Galileo using his telescope and can be seen now with just a pair of binoculars on a clear night.

FACT FILE

$$T = \frac{1}{f} \quad \omega = 2\pi f \quad v = r\omega$$

$$a = r\omega^2 \quad F = mr\omega^2$$

$$F = G\frac{M_1 M_2}{R^2} \quad V = -\frac{GM}{R}$$

$$g = -\frac{GM}{R^2}$$

where T = time period, f = frequency, ω = angular velocity, r = radius, a = acceleration, F = force, G = universal gravitational constant, M_1 and M_2 = masses a distance R apart, V = the gravitational potential at a distance R from a mass M, g = the gravitational field strength at a distance R from a mass M.

Volume of a sphere of radius $r = \frac{4}{3}\pi r^3$

$G = 6.7 \times 10^{-11}$ N m^2 kg^{-2}

1 From the table it can be seen that the satellite Io is very similar to that of the Moon.
   a) What are the main similarities and what are the differences?

b) Calculate the orbital speed of Io and the Moon.

2 The Moon is remarkable because we always see the same side facing the Earth.
   a) How does this happen?
   b) What is the period of rotation of the Moon about its own axis?

3 a) Plot a graph of (the period of orbit)^2 for the satellites of Jupiter against (the radius of orbit)^3.
   b) What does the graph tell you about the relationship between the period of orbit and the radius of orbit?
   c) Find out who discovered a similar law to the one you have just verified and what else he discovered.

4 A spacecraft makes an emergency landing on Titan.
   a) What local gravitational field strength do the astronauts experience? How will this affect their movements?
   b) What is the velocity that the spacecraft will have to achieve in order to escape from the satellite?

5 Find out about the problems that Galileo experienced as the result of his discoveries. Do scientists experience problems today getting their ideas accepted? If so how do they overcome this? Discuss.

6 a) A communications satellite is geostationary. What does this mean?
   b) Calculate the height above the Earth's surface of such a satellite.
   (Take $g = 10$ m s^{-2} and the radius of the Earth = 6378 km.)

7 Derive an equation to show where exactly a spacecraft would have to be between the Earth and the Moon in order to experience no net gravitational force from either the Moon or the Earth.

Safety first

After the recent fatalities caused by lightning striking an unprotected house, our newspaper is carrying out a local campaign to ensure that all houses are connected up to lightning conductors. According to our science correspondent a lightning conductor can actually reduce the likelihood of a strike by reducing the charge on the cloud above the conductor. Charge, opposite to the charge on the base of the cloud, streams upwards from the point of the conductor. This streaming will only occur if the conductor is properly connected to the earth. In our survey of one street in our town, two lightning conductors were found which were not properly connected to earth. We urge our readers to check their connections but not, we repeat not, during an actual thunderstorm.

Should you be so unlucky as to experience a direct strike on your house the conductor should ensure a safe path to earth for the current.

Lightning flashes are in fact quite complex events which occur due to the separation of charge in a thundercloud. A flash normally consists of several pulses of lightning. The initial stage includes a pilot leader which ionises a path to earth and which is followed by an immediate large transfer of charge in a return pulse. Repeated leaders and return pulses follow along the ionised path.

FACT FILE

The energy W in J of a charged capacitor $= \frac{1}{2}QV$ where Q = the charge stored in C and V = the potential difference between the plates in V.

1 Why is the connection to earth so important and why mustn't you check it out during a thunderstorm?

2 Explain the reference to a lightning conductor *reducing the charge* at the base of a thundercloud. How and why does this happen?
(Hint: find out about 'action at a point'.)

3 A thundercloud usually has quite strong thermals within it and can be 7000 m in height.
a) How might this contribute to the separation of charge within the cloud?
b) What are likely to be the charge carriers?

4 **a)** Why do you think the path of a pilot leader in lightning is rarely a dead straight line?
b) What are likely to be the charge carriers in a lightning flash?
c) Discuss how you think thunder is produced during a storm.

5 **a)** Calculate the energy released in a lightning flash if there is a potential difference of 10^{10} V between the base of the cloud and the earth and the charge passing through the flash is 5 C.
b) What assumptions have you made in your calculation?
c) What forms will the transferred energy take?

6 Find out about the early experiments performed by Franklin and Richmann in the eighteenth century. Richmann was killed and Franklin was lucky to escape with his life. Why were their experiments so dangerous?

7 In view of the dangers involved, consider safety precautions for walkers if caught out on the hills in a storm.

The wandering stars

From very early times people noticed the 'wandering' stars in the sky. Chinese astronomers many hundreds of years ago gathered data on planets or wandering stars and could also predict eclipses of the Sun and Moon accurately.

The table gives some of the data on the planets that have been calculated over the centuries.

Planet	Mean distance from Sun/10⁹m	Period of orbit/days	Radius /km	Density /kgm⁻³
Mercury	57.91	87.97	2420	5400
Venus	108.21	224.70	6100	5100
Earth	149.60	365.26	6378	5520
Mars	227.94	686.98	3380	3970
Jupiter	668.30	4332.59	71350	1330
Saturn	1427	10759.20	60400	680
Uranus	2869	30685	23800	1600
Neptune	4498	60188	22200	2250
Pluto	5900	90700	3000	Uncertain

FACT FILE

$$T = \frac{1}{f} \qquad \omega = 2\pi f \qquad v = r\omega$$

$$a = r\omega^2 \qquad F = mr\omega^2$$

$$F = G\frac{M_1 M_2}{R^2} \qquad V = -\frac{GM}{R}$$

$$g = -\frac{GM}{R^2}$$

where T = time period, f = frequency, ω = angular velocity, r = radius, a = acceleration, F = force, G = universal gravitational constance, M_1 and M_2 = masses a distance R apart, V = the gravitational potential at a distance R from a mass M, g = the gravitational field strength at a distance R from a mass M.

Volume of a sphere of radius r is $\frac{4}{3}\pi r^3$

$G = 6.7 \times 10^{-11}$ N m² kg⁻²

1 Why were the planets called wandering stars? Find out why they sometimes reverse direction in the sky for a while.

2 What conditions have to be satisfied to get:
   a) an eclipse of the Sun?
   b) an eclipse of the Moon?

3 From the data listed in the table, the planets divide into two distinct groups. What are the characteristics of each group?

4 Taking the orbits of the planets as approximately circular, calculate:
   a) the frequency of rotation round the Sun.
   b) the angular velocity of each planet in orbit.
   c) the speed of each planet in orbit.
   d) the centripetal acceleration of each planet towards the Sun.
   e) the force acting on each planet to hold it in orbit.

5 Given that the mass of the Sun is approximately 335 000 times that of the Earth, calculate an approximate value for the gravitational constant *G*.

6 a) Given that the received intensity of light from the Sun is inversely proportional to the square of a planet's distance from the Sun, calculate the ratio of the intensities received by:
  i) the Earth and Mars.
  ii) the Earth and Jupiter.
  b) What implications do these ratios have for the possibility of life on other planets?

7 In fact, on some planets the intensity of the received radiation is much less than would be calculated as in Question 6. Find out why.

8 a) The diameter of the Sun is 13.92 x 10⁵ km. Calculate the ratio of the local gravitational field strength at the surface of the Sun to that at the surface of the Earth.
  b) The observed acceleration of a falling body at the Earth's surface is less at the equator than at the poles. Assuming that the Earth is a perfect sphere give a possible reason for this. Given that the observed value of g at the pole is 9.81 m s⁻², calculate the value that would be observed at the equator.

9 a) Derive a formula for the escape velocity from a planet in terms of the mass of the planet *M*, the universal gravitational constant *G*, and the radius of the planet *R*.
  b) Calculate the escape velocity from Earth and from Mars.

30 UNDERGROUND CURRENT

Read the article on the opposite page and then answer the questions which follow.

FACT FILE

Current density $J = \dfrac{I}{A}$ where I = current in amps and A = the cross–sectional area in m². $J = nev$ where n = the number density of the charge carriers, e = the electronic charge in C and v = the drift velocity of the charge carriers in m s⁻¹.

1 In the article, mention is made of the alkaline fluids that are good conductors of electricity. Why do you think this is so and what do you think will be the main charge carriers in the fluid?

2 Describe why the currents may have been formed and give the laws that will predict the size and direction of the currents.

3 Suppose the average size of the current detected is 1 mA. Estimate the current density of current.

4 Given a drift velocity of only 10⁻⁴ m s⁻¹, as in ordinary conductors, estimate the number of charge carriers per cubic metre using your results to Question 3.

5 Why may the detection of such currents prove important in the future?

UNDERGROUND CURRENT ELECTRIFIES AUSTRALIA

The world's longest natural electric current has been discovered under Australia. The current passes through sedimentary rocks for more than 6000 kilometres across the Australian outback. Its nearest rival, some 2000 kilometres shorter, is a current running from Wyoming into Canada in North America.

Francois Chamalaun from Flinders University, who discovered the current, says that similar currents may exist under other continents. They could have been formed as the land masses collided hundreds of millions of years ago. According to Chamalaun, the current is induced by the Earth's ever-changing magnetic field.

In the most extensive geomagnetic survey carried out in Australia, the Bureau of Mineral Resources placed an array of 54 highly sensitive magnetometers in a grid across Australia. The instruments detected a weak electrical current between 15 and 45 kilometres below the surface. The width of the current varies between 50 and 2000 kilometres.

The current runs from the continental shelf off Broome in the far northwest of Western Australia, down into the north of South Australia, and then up through Queensland into the Gulf of Carpentaria. A side branch of the main current runs from near Birdsville in South Australia, through the Flinders Ranges, and into Spencer Gulf near Adelaide.

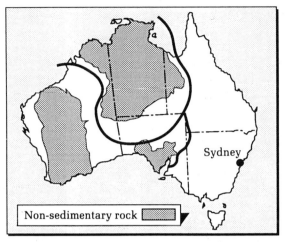

Non-sedimentary rock

Figure 30.1

The current runs along fracture zones in sedimentary basins. The fracture zones, which formed as ancient plates of the Earth's crust collided, contain alkaline fluids which conduct electricity well. The current is extremely weak. It would not provide enough power to light a lamp. But if the current was involved with the formation of the ancient sedimentary basins, as scientists believe, it may provide clues to deposits of oil and gas. It may also help to explain the geological origins of the Australian continent.

INK JET PRINTERS

These versatile printers depend on the deflection of falling charged ink drops by an electric field.

An ink jet printer has the advantages both that it is much quieter than a dot matrix printer and that complex characters can easily be produced through the computer control of the amount of charge on individual droplets of ink. A charging electrode in a gun producing the droplets is linked to a computer to ensure that each droplet is deflected the precise amount needed. Also by using different coloured ink cartridges it is easy to change the colour of the printing. The ink jet method allows for very fast printing.

FACT FILE

In a uniform electric field the field strength

$E = \dfrac{\Delta V}{\Delta x}$ and $\Delta W = Q\Delta V$ where V = the electric

potential, x = the distance, W = the electric potential energy and Q = the charge

1 Why are the ink jet printers nearly silent?

2 **a)** Why must the charge on each droplet be precisely controlled?
   b) If the droplets are falling between two vertical plates, separated by a distance d, with a potential diffence V between them, draw a diagram to show the forces acting on an individual drop of mass m.

3 An experiment was demonstrated in the laboratory to illustrate the action of an ink jet printer. A potential difference of 2 kV to 5 kV was put across a gap between two vertical plates. Ink drops were allowed to fall from a syringe which was also connected to the positive terminal of the E.H.T. supply.
   a) If paper was pulled along under the plates at right angles to the field set up, what would be seen if the voltage was varied?
   b) What would be seen if the voltage was switched off?

4 If in the experiment in Question 3 an ink drop had a mass of 0.1 g and a charge of 40 nC and the p.d. between the plates was 2 kV:
   a) calculate the sideways force on the ink drop while between the plates, if the plate separation is 10 cm.
   b) state the downward force on the drop (neglecting air resistance and Archemedian upthrust).
   c) calculate the length of time the ink drop is falling between the plates, if each vertical plate has a depth of 5 cm.

5 Now, using the data in Question 4 calculate:
   a) the deflection of the drop on leaving the plates.
   b) the deflection of the drop when it strikes the paper, if the paper is 10 cm below the bottom of the plates.

6 The demonstration described in Question 3 is rather dangerous.
   a) What safety precautions would have to be observed?
   b) What safety precautions would manufacturers of such printers have to incorporate?

Cleaning up the air we breathe

No longer should our factories be belching forth smoke and grime. Dust precipitators installed in chimneys can cut the emission of smoke particles to almost zero (they can be 99% efficient). Large earthed vertical metal plates are installed in the factory chimney and high voltage vertical wires are installed between the plates. In the resultant strong electrical field the air round the wires becomes ionised. The positive ions are attracted to the wires and the electrons repelled. The electrons are attracted to the dust particles in the smoke which are then attracted to the plates. The plates are periodically vibrated to get the accumulated dust to the bottom of the factory chimney.

*F*ACT *FILE*

Electric field lines start on a positively–charged body and end on a negatively–charged body. Electric field lines concentrate in areas of stronger field.

1 In the factory dust precipitator described above, the voltage applied to the central wires is around 50 kV. State with reasons:
a) whether this voltage is positive or negative with respect to earth.
b) whether the earthed plates are positive or negative with respect to the central wires.

2 Draw a cross–section of the chimney and show the electric field lines. Indicate where the field will be strongest and how different ions and particles will be moving.

3 Some dust particles end up on the central wires rather than at the plates. What will have happened to them?

IONISER MONITORS AND CLEANS THE AIR

Ionisers emit negative ions to counteract dirt, dust, pollution and static electricity in the air. But sometimes positive ions are required as well to restore optimum ion balance and create a perfect 'natural' environment indoors. The superb Home Ioniser/Air Purifier we're offering here achieves this by emitting both positive and negative ions, as well as actually cleaning the air through its removable washable filter. Mains powered (adaptor supplied), it measures $6^{1}/_{4}$" x $3^{1}/_{2}$". Also available is our popular (and surprisingly inexpensive) In-Car Ioniser. It is $4^{3}/_{4}$" long, and simply plugs into the car lighter socket.
Home Ioniser/Air Purifier £24.95 UE635A
In-Car Ioniser £14.95 UE392D

4 a) In the home ioniser advertisement, both positive and negative ions are going into the room. How do you think this might be achieved?
b) A washable filter appears to be collecting the dust in the home ioniser. How might this be achieved?

5 It is particularly important to remove sulphur dioxide from chimney emissions. The dust precipitator does not achieve this although it can remove solid sulpur particles. Why is this so?

6 How do the ionisers in the advertisement 'counteract dirt, dust, pollution and static electricity in the air'? Discuss.

33 ▶ INSIDE THE ATOM

Atoms make up everything and scientists recognise the importance of having a clear idea of what makes up an atom. Atoms cannot be seen directly but scientists put forward different models of the atom based on indirect experimental evidence. Rutherford's model of the nuclear atom was postulated in 1911 as the result of Geiger and Marsden's experiments bombarding gold foil. The model suggested that every atom contained a compact positively–charged nucleus with negatively–charged electrons orbiting round it. The nucleus was supposed to have a radius of 10^{-15} m and the electrons were supposed to orbit in a sphere of radius 10^{-10} m.

There were problems with this model because scientists realised that the orbiting electrons were accelerated electric charges. This means that they lose energy by radiating electromagnetic waves and so spiral inwards.

FACT FILE

$F = G\dfrac{M_1 M_2}{R^2}$ where G = the universal gravitational constant, i.e. 6.67×10^{-11} N kg^{-2}m^2 and M_1 and M_2 = masses a distance R apart.

$F = \dfrac{Q_1 Q_2}{4\pi\varepsilon_o R^2}$ where ε_o = the permittivity of free space, i.e. 8.85×10^{-12} F m^{-1} and Q_1 and Q_2 = charges a distance R apart.
e = electronic charge, i.e. 1.60×10^{-19} C
Mass of an electron = 9.11×10^{-31} kg
Mass of a proton = 1.673×10^{-27} kg
Mass of a neutron = 1.675×10^{-27} kg

1 The article says atoms cannot be seen, but what about the action of electron microscopes? Discuss.

2 a) Describe Geiger and Marsden's experiment. How did it support Rutherford's model?

b) Estimate the density of an atom of helium and the density of a nucleus of helium. What does this tell you about the space in an atom?
c) Find out about how neutron stars are formed.

3 If the orbiting electrons lose energy, what will happen to:
a) their position?
b) their speed?
(Hint: consider both the electron's potential energy in the electric field of the nucleus and its kinetic energy.)

4 a) In a hydrogen atom, what is the attractive force on an electron in Rutherford's nuclear model due to:
i) the electrostatic attraction?
ii) the gravitational attraction?
b) Which force will play the dominant role in the model?

5 There is evidence that the nucleus of a helium atom is very stable.
a) What is this evidence?
b) Estimate the electrostatic force between the two protons in a helium nucleus.
c) Now estimate the gravitational force between the two protons in a helium nucleus.
d) From your calculations what ought to happen to the two protons?

6 From the calculations in Question 5 a new force had to be postulated to account for nucleons staying together in the nucleus. Find out the name of this force and its characteristics.

7 As the Rutherford nuclear model was flawed it was eventually replaced by the Bohr model. Compare and contrast these two models.

Read the passage below and then answer the questions on the following page.

Early experimenters with electrostatic machines regarded working with electricity as an interesting activity which generated showy demonstrations but which would never have any real use! They did discover, however, that they could achieve much bigger sparks if they incorporated a long rod of iron into their design. Somehow it seemed to allow them to build up more charge before a spark developed. This idea of storing charge was developed by Pieter van Musschenbroek who stored charge in a hand held bottle of water containing a brass wire. This idea was later developed into the Leyden jar, two of which can be seen in the photograph of the Wimshurst machine. These are glass jars with an inner and outer coating of metal foil. The outer coating was earthed by standing the jar on a table or holding it.

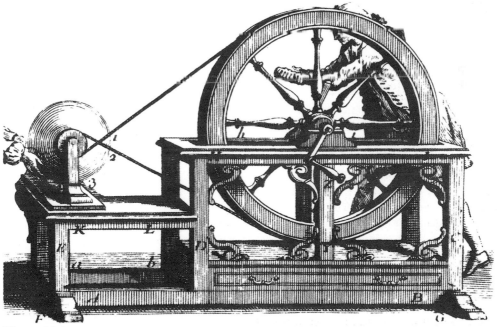

Figure 34.1

$C = \dfrac{Q}{V}$ where C = the capacitance, Q = the charge and V = the electric potential difference.

For a parallel plate capacitor $C = \dfrac{\varepsilon_o \varepsilon_r A}{d}$ where A = the area of a plate in m², d = the separation of the plates in m, ε_o = the permittivity of free space, ε_r = the relative permittivity of the medium between the plates.

Permittivity of free space = 8.85×10^{-12} F m⁻¹

Capacitors in parallel $C = C_1 + C_2 + C_3 \dots$

Capaciters in series $\dfrac{1}{C} = \dfrac{1}{C_1} + \dfrac{1}{C_2} + \dfrac{1}{C_3} \dots$

The energy of a charged capacitor $W = \dfrac{1}{2}QV$

where Q = the charge stored and V = the potential difference between the plates.

1 What was happening when the early experimenters used a long iron rod? Discuss.

2 The Leyden jar was one of the earliest forms of capacitor. Explain how it worked in terms of what you know about capacitors.

3 a) Two parallel metal plates are set up opposite each other. One plate is charged and the other plate is earthed. What happens to the capacitance and the potential between the plates if:

(i) the plates of a parallel capacitor are brought closer together but the overlapping area is kept the same?

(ii) the plates are kept the same distance apart but the area of overlap of the plates is increased?

(iii) the plates have a piece of wax inserted between them?

b) How might you give a simple laboratory demonstration to show how the potential changes?

4 How do you think the design and use of the Leyden jars was improved to give bigger sparks?

5 Imagine you have six Leyden jars. To get the maximum possible charge stored do you connect them in series with the electric machine or connect them in parallel? Justify your answer.

6 A 5 µF capacitor is charged up to a p.d. of 10 V. It is then removed from the charging circuit and connected across an uncharged 2 µF capacitor. Calculate:

a) the initial charge and energy stored in the 5 µF capacitor.

b) the final p.d. across the combination.

c) the energy stored by the capacitors at the end. Why is this less than you started with?

7 a) If you have four capacitors of 100 µF each and each having a working voltage of 6 V, what is the best way to arrange them with a 12 V battery so that they store the maximum amount of charge?

b) What is the total charge stored?

35 METERING

Without meters, we would be unable to measure electric currents and voltages. Accurate measurement and control of electricity is a keystone to our way of life today.

1 The statements in the above paragraph are rather sweeping! Do you agree? Discuss and justify.

2 A moving coil ammeter needs alternative shunts in parallel with the coil to enable different current ranges to be measured. A particular ammeter has a coil of resistance 10 Ω and a full scale deflection when the current through the coil is 50 mA. Calculate the shunt needed for the meter to read a range of:
  a) 0 – 1 A.
  b) 0 – 5 A.
  c) 0 – 10 A.
  d) 0 – 50 A.

3 A moving coil voltmeter needs alternative resistors in series with the coil to enable different voltage ranges to be measured. The alternative resistors are called multipliers. A particular voltmeter has a coil of resistance 10 Ω and a full scale deflection when the current through the coil is 50 mA. Calculate the multiplier needed for the meter to read a range of:
  a) 0 – 1 V.
  b) 0 – 5 V.
  c) 0 – 10 V.
  d) 0 – 50 V.

4 Draw a circuit diagram for a multimeter with the same coil characteristics as described in Questions 2 and 3, showing how the switching can achieve the different ranges given.

5 a) How can a.c. be measured using a multimeter?
  b) Sketch a circuit diagram to show how the multimeter must be adapted.
  c) Is the value of the a.c. measured the peak value or the r.m.s. value?

Cosmic rays are streams of fast–moving charged particles constantly bombarding the Earth from outer space. They give rise to much of the background ionisation detected on Earth when experimenting with radioactivity.

The cosmic rays interact with the Earth's magnetic field and are deflected away from the equator towards the poles. The Earth's field also traps cosmic ray particles in zones above the Earth. The Van Allen radiation belts were discovered by the American Explorer satellites in 1958. These radiation belts, which contain both high energy electrons and protons, pose dangers for astronauts and as a result it is vital that the Earth's magnetic field is properly mapped in space. Satellite magnetometers are used to measure the strength of the field. The magnetometers use Hall probes as these are simple in construction and relatively robust and compact.

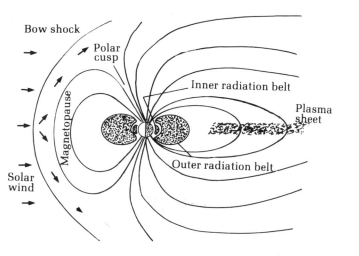

Figure 36.1

FACT FILE

Hall effect voltage $V_h = \dfrac{BI}{ntq}$ where B = the magnetic field strength in T, I = the current in A, n = the charge carrier number density, t = the thickness of the conductor in m and q = the charge of each carrier in C.

1 How will a positively–charged particle travel in a uniform magnetic field if:
   a) its initial velocity is perpendicular to the field direction?
   b) its initial velocity is at 30° to the field direction?

2 With reference to the map of the Earth's magnetic field:
   a) discuss why cosmic rays are more intense at the poles than at the equator.
   b) consider why some particles get trapped in the Van Allen belts.
   c) discuss why such particles might pose a danger to astronauts.

3 a) Find out what causes the solar wind shown on the diagram in Fig.36.1.

b) What does the solar wind appear to do to the Earth's magnetic field?

c) What effect do you think might be observed during increased sun spot activity on the Sun?

4 a) The Hall effect voltage is given by the formula in the fact file. Derive this formula by considering the forces on the charge carriers in the slab of semiconductor material.

b) What does the direction of the Hall voltage tell you about the charge carriers?

c) The Hall effect was known about long before semiconductor materials were discovered. Why was it not considered to be of any particular use at that time?

5 Calculate the Hall voltage that develops when a Hall probe is in the Earth's magnetic field at a point where the magnetic flux density B is 80 μT. (The probe contains a piece of semiconductor material of thickness 5 mm, a charge carrier density of 1×10^{24} m^{-3}, a charge on the carriers of 1.6×10^{-19} C, and carries a current of 100 mA.)

6 How can Hall probes be calibrated to measure the strength of unknown magnetic fields?

7 Why does the Hall probe have such big advantages over old–fashioned magnetometers?

37 TELEVISION

Read the articles below and on the following page and then answer the questions which follow.

Television is arguably the most influential invention of this century. Nations are determined, wars and politics influenced and personal development changed by this invention. The actual mechanics of how a television works is relatively simple.

In a black and white television, an electron gun sends a stream of electrons to a fluorescent screen. The brightness of the spot at any one moment will determine the effect seen. The spot is made to scan the entire screen in 1/25 of a second. During this time it travels across the screen 625 times at a steady speed, flying back almost instantaneously between sweeps. The spot is deflected across the screen by magnetic deflecting coils and at the same time another pair of coils gradually moves the spot down the screen.

In a colour television there are three electron guns giving three streams of electrons. The screen is now coated with alternating dots of phosphor which glow either red, green or blue when struck by an electron beam. Between the gun and the screen there is a grid of tiny holes so that each electron stream strikes the correct colour dots. The beams are scanned across the screen in the same way as before and a colour picture is built up.

'BLACK TRINITRON'

Sony has never rested on its laurels, in spite of numerous industry awards and even an Emmy from the US Academy of Television Arts and Sciences. Flatter tubes can increase reflective glare, but this is countered by a further improvement to 'Trinitron' technology called 'Black Trinitron'. By adding light-absorbent black carbon stripes to the inside of the tube, reflection and eye fatigue have been effectively minimised.

'Black Trinitron' can only perform to its full potential in conjunction with the 'Trinitron' patented low distortion cylindrical screen. In order to maximise the performance of large screen sizes of 25" (59cm Visible FST) and above, 'Black Trinitron' is supplemented by 'Microblack Trinitron', a further refined version of the well-known Sony Aperture Grille, the advanced system through which colour beams are sorted.

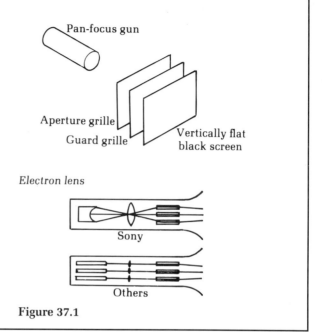

Figure 37.1

Black Trinitron and Trinitron Plus are trademarks of the Sony Corporation

FACT FILE

Force on an electron in a magnetic field $F = Bev$ where B = the magnetic field strength in T, e = the electronic charge in C and v = the electron speed in m s^{-1}.
$e = 1.6 \times 10^{-19}$ C

1 The effects of television are discussed in the first article. Do you agree with what is said? Discuss.

2 **a)** How must the magnetic field be orientated to give the small deflection needed to send the electron beam across the screen?
b) What is the force on an electron moving with a speed of 3×10^7 m s^{-1} at right angles to a field where $B = 2 \times 10^{-3}$ T?

c) What is the force if the electron is travelling initially at an angle of 30° to the field?

3 How will the brightness of the spot from the electron gun be controlled?

4 **a)** According to the second article how does the grid in a Sony colour television differ from other makes (see Fig.37.1)?
b) If a magnet is brought near a colour television, the shape of the picture is temporarily altered and permanent colour distortion results. (**Do not do this!**) The distortion can only be removed by getting the screen degaussed. What has happened and how is it being cured?
c) The distorting effect is not permanent if a magnet is brought up to a black and white set. Why?

5 a) Estimate:
   (i) how long it takes an electron beam to travel across a 25" TV screen.
   (ii) the speed of the electron beam across the screen.
   b) What assumptions have you made?

6 Suppose the beam was being deflected by a pair of plates providing a uniform electric field. Sketch a graph of the voltage against time that would need to be applied to the plates to ensure the correct motion of the spot across the screen.

38   X-RAYS

Appeal for CT scanner

Hambleton hospital had a surprise when they needed to treat Linda Davies. The X-ray equipment, a CT scanner, needed to investigate her condition was only available at the County Hospital 60 miles away. Linda was so incensed by all the travel and worry this caused that she set in motion the Hambleton Hospital scanner appeal. Now, two years later, a cheque for £300 000 has been given to the Hospital for this important piece of equipment.

Linda explained to our reporter that the CT scanner would enable more detailed pictures of soft tissue within the body to be seen by using a technique called computer tomography. Slices of the body are examined in turn by X-rays and unwanted reflections from other parts of the body are eliminated by computer analysis. Linda assures us that no actual slicing occurs and the technique is quite pleasant to experience.

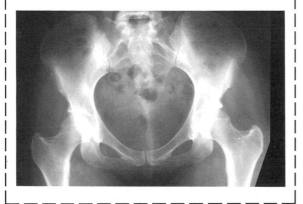

*F*ACT FILE

The maximum energy of an electron striking the target in an X-ray tube $E_{max} = eV_o$ where e = the electronic charge in C and V_o = the peak voltage across the tube in V.
The energy of an X-ray photon $E = hf$ joules where h = Planck constant and f = the frequency in Hz.
$e = 1.6 \times 10^{-19}$ C; $h = 6.6 \times 10^{-34}$ Js

1 Why do you think the CT scanner is needed instead of an ordinary X-ray tube to get details of tissue structure ?

2 A typical modern X-ray tube has a peak potential difference of 100 kV across it.
   a) Calculate the maximum energy of an electron striking the target.
   b) Calculate the maximum frequency of the emitted X-rays. What assumption have you made in your calculation?
   c) Calculate the minimum wavelength of the emitted X-rays.
   d) What will happen to the graph shown in Fig. 38.1 if the voltage across the tube is increased?

3 a) What are the spikes on the graph in Fig.38.1 due to?
b) What happens to these spikes if the voltage across the tube is increased?
c) What happens to them if the material of the target is changed?

4 a) A modern X-ray tube has a rotating anode. Why do you think this is necessary?
b) The tube is also evacuated and encased in lead. What are the reasons for each of these measures?

5 Why can't X-rays be easily focussed?

6 See if you can find out more about CT scanners and how they work.

7 Another way to get a better X-ray picture is to use an image intensifier. See if you can find out how one works.

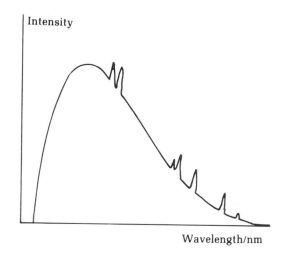

Figure 38.1

39 **INDUCTION HOBS**

Look at the advertisement on the opposite page and then answer the following questions.

$\boldsymbol{F}$ACT FILE

$\dfrac{N_s}{N_p} = \dfrac{V_s}{V_p}$ where N_s = the number of turns on a secondary coil, N_p = the number of turns on a primary coil, V_s = the voltage across the secondary coil and V_p = the voltage across the primary coil.

$Z = \sqrt{R^2 + (\omega L)^2}$ where Z = the impedance of a circuit, R = the resistance, and ωL = the inductive reactance.

1 Why is the picture of a permanent magnet in the advertisement somewhat misleading? Explain what you would expect to find underneath the *induction* hob surface.

2 *The moment a pan is placed on the hob it creates a magnetic field.* Discuss this statement from the advertisement. What does 'it' in the statement refer to? What sort of magnetic field will be created? Where does it originate and how far do you think it will extend ?

3 What will happen in the base of the pan as a result of being on the hob? Discuss the reasons for this.

Wha on eart   makes an induct on hob so ea y to control?

At first glance, an induction hob looks much like any ceramic hob. It has the same sleek good looks. The same wipe-clean surface. Under the heating area, however, sits a powerful electric magnet. The moment you place a metal pan on the hob it creates a magnetic field. This, in turn, sets up heating currents in the pan.

As no heat is lost on the hob surface, the food starts cooking immediately. (Even on maximum output, the hob hardly feels warm to the touch.)

With such a rapid response, you can regulate the heat precisely, from a gentle simmer to a sizzling stir-fry.

Now do you see the attraction?

COOKELECTRIC

4 Why do you think the hob feels hardly warm to the touch, even on maximum output?

5 What sort of pans will you need to use on an induction hob and why?

6 The effectiveness of an induction hob is greatly reduced if the base of the pan is warped. Why should this be so?

7 A very simple model of the situation is that of a transformer with a secondary coil consisting of a single loop.

  a) Why is this a very simplistic model?
  b) Using the model and the data below, calculate or state:
    (i) the power supplied to the primary.
    (ii) the r.m.s. voltage across the secondary loop.
    (iii) the r.m.s. current in the secondary coil assuming 100% efficiency.

Power rating = 500 W. r.m.s. voltage across primary = 240 V. Number of turns in the primary coil = 12.

8 The currents flowing in the base of the pan are unlikely to be as big as this given that the pan will have a sizable impedance to the flow of the current. If the r.m.s. voltage across such a circuit is 35 V when an r.m.s. current of 5 A flows calculate:

  a) the impedance of the circuit.
  b) the inductance of such a circuit if the frequency of the mains supply is 50 Hz and the resistance is 6 Ω.
  c) the heat developed in such a circuit.

9 Why don't you get an electric shock if you inadvisedly touch the pan while it is on the hob?

Read the article below and then answer the questions which follow.

THE IDEA OF ELECTRIC POWER AND SUPPLY

[Sir W. Siemens writes to his brother William, on December 4th, 1866.]

I have had a new idea, which, in all probability will succeed and will give important results.

As you well know Wilde has taken a patent in England consisting in the combination of a magnet-inductor* of my construction with a second one which has a large electromagnet instead of the steel magnet. The magnet inductor as constructed in our alphabetical telegraph instruments, magnetises the electro-magnet to a higher degree than can be obtained by steel magnets. The second inductor will therefore give much more powerful currents than if it had steel magnets. The action ought to be colossal, as is stated in *Dingler's Journal*.

But now, clearly, the magnet-inductor with steel magnets may be entirely dispensed with. If we take an electro-magnetic machine, which is so constructed that the stationary magnet is an electro-magnet with a constant polar direction, while the current of the movable magnet is changed; and if we insert a small battery,† which will thus work the apparatus, and now turn the machine in the contrary direction the current must increase. The battery may (then) be excluded and removed. . . .

We may thereby with the sole aid of wire-coils and soft iron transform power into current.

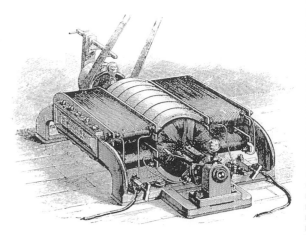

. . .Magneto-electricity will by this means become cheap and electric lighting, galvanometallurgy,‡ and even small electromagnetic machines§ receiving their power from larger ones will become possible and useful.

(Life of Sir W. Siemens. W. Pole. 1888. p.233.)

* i.e. a dynamo with permanent steel magnets.
† This proved to be unnecessary.
‡ i.e. electro-plating, large scale electrolysis, etc.
§ i.e. Electric motors.

*F*ACT FILE

e.m.f. produced in a coil rotating in a uniform magnetic field $E = BAN\omega\sin \omega t$ where B = the magnetic flux density in T, ω = the angular speed of the coil in rads^{-1}, N = the number of turns, A = the cross–sectional area of the coil in m^2 and t = the time in seconds from the start.

$\dfrac{N_s}{N_p} = \dfrac{V_s}{V_p}$ where N_s = the number of turns on a secondary coil, N_p = the number of turns on a primary coil, V_s = the voltage across the secondary coil and V_p = the voltage across the primary coil.

1 Read the article carefully and then describe the generator that Siemens is proposing.

2 Why was the battery unnecessary? Explain. (What is really fascinating here is that Siemens thought it might be necessary in the first place!)

3 What advantages did Siemens see for society with the development of his generator?

4 Why is the soft iron considered to be more effective than the steel?

5 **a)** What would increase the e.m.f. produced by a dynamo or generator?
b) What is the maximum e.m.f. produced by a dynamo with a coil of 100 turns and an area 10 cm^2, if it is rotated at a frequency of 50 Hz in a magnetic flux density of 0.01 T.
c) What is the position of the coil when the maximum e.m.f. occurs? Explain why this is so.

d) What is the frequency of the e.m.f. produced?

6 To deliver the power from the generators used today, power losses are minimised by transmitting at very high voltages and using transformers to achieve this.
a) Find out about the different voltages used in the National Grid and the Super Grid.
b) Electricity is stepped down from 11 000 V at substations to 240 V for domestic use.
(**i**) Calculate the turns ratio needed for the transformers.
(**ii**) A housing estate of 500 houses is served by one such substation. If, when *Neighbours* finishes on the television, every household switches on a 3 kW electric kettle to make a cup of tea, calculate the current drawn from the supply cables to the substation if the transformers are 99% efficient.

41 TUNING CIRCUITS

Read the following passage and then answer the questions which follow

To tune in to your favourite radio station you will be using a variable band selector and a series tuning circuit in your radio. The capacitor is in parallel with an inductor in the band selector or aerial balancing circuit. Signals of many different frequencies arrive at the aerial and adjusting the circuit enables you to pick out the band you want. Low frequency signals pass through the inductor to Earth and an irritating low hum is eliminated. High-frequency signals pass through the capacitance to Earth and a high-frequency hiss is eliminated. The remaining frequencies pass to the series tuning circuit. This is used to select a precise frequency. If the capacitor is adjusted to the precise value to give resonance in the series circuit at the frequency you want then you will tune into your station. The frequency you are after is the carrier frequency for your radio station.

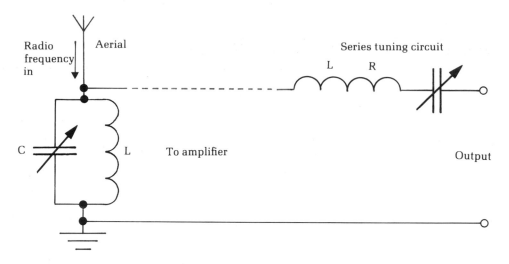

Figure 41.1

1 By considering the reactance of an inductor,
explain why low–frequency signals pass
through the inductor to Earth in the aerial
balancing circuit.

2 By considering the reactance of a capacitor,
explain why high–frequency signals pass
through the capacitor to Earth in the aerial
balancing circuit.

3 Show that, for an LCR series circuit,

resonance will occur when $f = \dfrac{1}{2\pi\sqrt{LC}}$ where

L = the inductance of the inductor and
C = the capacitance of the capacitor.

4 What is meant by carrier frequency in radio
transmission?

5 You want to tune in to Radio 4 long wave
and the wavelength you need is 1500 m.
Your series circuit contains an inductor of
inductance 50 nH. Calculate the value of the
capacitor needed to tune in to Radio 4.

6 a) A series circuit contains a coil of
resistance 20 Ω and inductance 30 mH, and
a capacitor of 100 μF. An r.m.s. current of
40 mA and frequency 50 Hz is passed
through the series circuit. Calculate:
   (i) the peak value of the current in the circuit.
   (ii) the peak p.d. across the coil.
   (iii) the peak p.d. across the capacitor.
   (iv) the peak p.d. across the coil and the
   capacitor.
   b) Why is the value you calculated in a) (iv)
not equal to the sum of the two values in
a) (ii) + (iii)?

7 Calculate the resonant frequency for the
circuit described in Question 6.

Read the article and then answer the questions which follow.

DIODES AND CAPACITORS: IMITATE TRANSFORMERS

The diode-capacitor network of Figure 42.1 accepts low current at a high voltage and delivers higher current at a lower voltage, behaving like a step-down transformer. You drive the circuit with a square-wave input signal as shown.

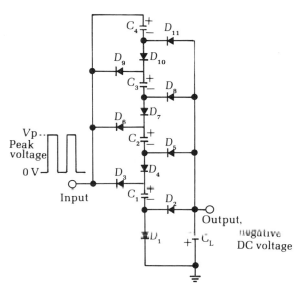

Figure 42.1 This diode-capacitor network converts an input square wave to a negative d.c. voltage.

When the input is at its peak voltage V_p, current through D_{10}, D_7, D_4 and D_1 charges the series capacitors C_4, C_3, C_2, and C_1. The voltage on each capacitor reaches approximately $1/4(V_p - 4V_F)$, where V_F is the forward-voltage drop across one diode.

However, the total output voltage doesn't equal the sum of the voltages on the four capacitors; it's less than that by two diode drops. Consequently, the circuit is inefficient for low-amplitude drive signals (too much voltage is lost across the diodes).

For 15V and 60V p-p inputs, the circuit's corre-

sponding outputs are approximately –1.65V and –12.9V, depending on the load. An input of 28V p-p produces about –5V. Notice that the square-wave generator must sink more current than it sources: It charges the capacitors in series, but discharges them in parallel.

When the input terminal switches to 0V, it connects the capacitors in parallel by pulling the positive side of each capacitor near 0V. The capacitor voltages then produce a current flow that creates a negative charge across the load capacitor (C_L). The voltages on C_3, C_2, and C_1, each charge C_L through two diodes in series, but the charging path through C_4 has only one Diode D_{11}. This configuration results in a higher surge current through D_{11} and C_4 and a slightly higher negative output voltage, unless you add a diode in series with D_{11}.

You can change the output voltage by adding or subtracting sections; C_1, D_1, D_3, and D_2 constitute one section, for example. Make the series capacitors equal in value and the total value of these capacitors equal to the load capacitor: $C_L = I/2V_R f$, where I is the load current, V_R is the maximum allowed p-p ripple voltage, and f is the input frequency.

DC TRANSFORMER

Here is an intriguing circuit which provides a low voltage high current output from a high voltage low (mean) current source. The nominal transformation ratio n in the instance shown is 4:1 step down, but unlike some other voltage-changing schemes using capacitors, n can be any whole number; it is not limited to powers of 2. This advantage apart, the circuit is of limited practical use as the efficiency is not too high due to all the diode drops. But one day someone will invent the perfect rectifier, and then.

Rudy Stefenel, Luma Telecom

FACT FILE

$Q = CV$

$\Sigma E = \Sigma V$ (Kirchhoff's second law)

1 a) The heading towards the end of the article says 'DC transformer' but what must be special about the d.c., if this does mean direct current, for the system to work?
b) What is the r.m.s. value of the supply voltage?

2 a) Explain why in this circuit, the capacitors are charged in series and discharged in parallel. Draw the circuit diagrams in each case to show what is happening.

b) What implication, stated in the article, does this have for the signal wave generator and why?

3 a) Explain why you think the voltage on each capacitor reaches only approximately $\frac{1}{4}(V_P - 4V_F)$ rather than $\frac{1}{4}V_P$.
b) Why is the output voltage negative and less than a $\frac{1}{4}V_P$ by two diode drops?
c) For each of the input and output voltages given in the article calculate the value of V_F.

4 a) How can the circuit be extended and what might limit how far the extension can go?
b) Why do people still strive to invent the perfect rectifier?

43 ▶ USING A CAT TO FIND BURIED CABLES

Read the brochure on the opposite page carefully and then answer the questions on the following page.

The CAT (cable avoiding tool) contains dual channel sensors. Pre amps and filters produce two signal strengths that are compared to determine if the CAT is directly above the conductor. The comparator controls the passage of the signal to the loudspeaker.

FACT FILE

$B = \dfrac{\mu_o I}{2\pi a}$ where B = the magnetic flux density, I = the current in a straight cable, and a = the perpendicular distance from the cable.

$E = -N\dfrac{d\phi}{dt}$ or the magnitude of the induced e.m.f. is proportional to the rate of change of the flux linkage.

1 In the P search mode, live cables can be detected.
a) What frequencies do most live cables carry?
b) Why do you think metal pipes and other cables can be detected near to live cables?

2 In the R search mode, cables that are not live can be detected. How is this done?

3 a) What is the process involved that causes a current to flow in a search coil when it is near a live cable?
b) Describe how a search coil in the CAT works.
c) Why should twin search coils locate the position of a buried cable more accurately than a single search coil?

4 The CAT is very directional and rejects interference from overhead power lines. How do you think this might be done?

Alone, the C.A.T finds buried metal pipes and cables. Add the Genny to trace and identify them.

The C.A.T and Genny are tools to solve everyday problems locating pipes, cables and metal covers in the highway before excavation.

The C.A.T was introduced seven years ago. User experience throughout the world has been fed back continuously into design resulting in steady improvement in product performance and service reliability.

The equipment is very simple to use and is designed for workmen who are not accustomed to using instruments. However its sensitivity and directionality gives it outstanding detection performance which will be fully appreciated by technicians.

The C.A.T alone with its two detection modes is an avoiding tool. It sweeps an area to locate buried metal pipes and cables.

When used with the Genny the C.A.T becomes a very discriminating mains finder and pipe and cable tracer.

The Genny when included a mode for locating lost metal covers.

The C.A.T and Genny replace three conventional locating instruments. The combination of three functions in a single set of equipment results in exceptional versatility to solve a wide range of location problems.

Alone the C.A.T locates buried metal pipes and cables

Originally called the Cable Avoiding Tool, the C.A.T sweeps an area to detect buried cables and other conductors before digging.

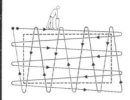

The C.A.T has *two search modes*. In the **P** search mode the C.A.T locates loaded power cables radiating 50/60Hz energy signals. These signals transfer naturally to other nearby cables and metal pipes which are also detected in the **P** mode.

The **R** mode is a new search mode which enables the C.A.T to detect long buried cables and buried metal pipes even though they do not carry any energy of their own. The **R** signals originate from distant VLF (Very Low Frequency) radio transmitters whose energy penetrates soil to reach buried conductors which re-radiate the signals in sufficient strength to be detected by the C.A.T.

The **P** and **R** search modes are complementary. They detect main cables and most other buried conductors: the combination of the two search modes enables the C.A.T to detect more buried conductors than conventional single mode locators.

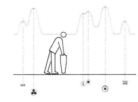

The C.A.T's twin search coil gives a very *narrow response* directly over the signal, thus enabling the position of separate but adjacent conductors to be located.

The C.A.T is very directional and *rejects interference* from sources such as overhead power lines; the C.A.T can be used in areas where conventional locators are ineffective.

The C.A.T is a very sensitive locator. It will detect the signal resulting from a pure power frequency current of less than 7.5 milliamps at 40 inches (1 metre) distance. Because power cables carry harmonic multiples of power frequencies, the effective sensitivity is even higher, so that currents as low as 2.5mA are detectable at this distance. The combination of sensitivity and discrimination makes the C.A.T the ideal tool for sweeping to locate buried metal pipes and cables.

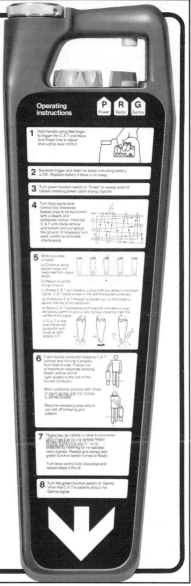

Operating instructions — P Power — R Radio — G Genny

1 Hold handle using little finger to trigger the C.A.T and leave fore-finger free to adjust blue signal level control.

2 Squeeze trigger and listen for bleep indicating battery is OK. Replace battery if there is no bleep.

3 Turn green function switch to 'Power' to sweep area for cables radiating power cable energy signals.

4 Turn blue signal level control fully clockwise. Sweep area to be excavated with a steady and deliberate motion. Hold the C.A.T with blade vertical and bottom end just above the ground. If necessary turn back control to eliminate interference.

5 When you hear a signal.
(a) Continue along search route until response from signal stops.
(b) Return to centre of signal level.
(c) Rotate C.A.T as if blade is a pivot until you detect a minimum signal. C.A.T blade is now in line with the buried conductor.
(d) Rotate the C.A.T through a quarter turn so that blade is across the line of the conductor.
(e) Move C.A.T backwards and forwards and reduce blue sensitivity control to give a very narrow response over the centre of the signal.
(f) C.A.T is now over the buried conductor with blade at right angles to it.

6 Track buried conductor keeping C.A.T vertical and moving it steadily from side to side. Follow line of maximum response keeping blade vertical and at right angles to the line of the buried conductor.
Mark conductor position with chalk or, better, leave end of area to end of area.
Resume sweeping area where you left off following grid pattern.

7 There may be cables or other buried metal conductors which are not radiating power signals but are radiating re-radiated radio signals. Repeat grid sweep with green function switch turned to Radio.
Turn blue control fully clockwise and repeat steps 4 thru 6.

8 Turn the green function switch to 'Genny' when the C.A.T is used to detect the Genny signal.

---

5 a) The current produced in the search coil depends on the current in the buried cable. What factors will determine the size of the current in the search coil?
b) Why do power cables carry harmonic multiples of power frequencies and why will this improve the effective sensitivity of the CAT?

6 a) A cable carries a peak current of 5 A and is buried at 0.5 m. What is the maximum magnetic flux density at the surface if μ_0 is $4\pi \times 10^{-7}$ Wb A^{-1} m^{-1}?
b) What is the e.m.f. induced in a search coil of 200 turns when the magnetic flux threading it changes at a uniform rate from 10 mWb to zero in 0.2 s?

7 a) Draw a flow diagram to show how the CAT operates.

b) An operational amplifier can be used as a voltage comparator between two signals. Draw a diagram of the circuit that would be needed and explain how it works.

8 In the CAT, a comparator that is a two input logic unit which gives a 1 at the output if the two inputs are the same as each other could be used. Such a comparator can be designed using six NAND gates. Draw the circuit needed and construct the truth table for the combination.

44 USING A SIGNAL TO HELP FIND CABLES

Read the brochure on the opposite page and then answer the questions which follow.

When the Genny is used to apply a signal, the very distinctive bleep can be heard in the street. If you hear this, go and have a look at the way the equipment is being used. As long as you don't get in the way you may well find that the search for cables is explained to you by the person working on the job.

*F*ACT FILE

$I_{r.m.s.} = \dfrac{I_o}{\sqrt{2}}$ for a sinusoidal wave where

I = the alternating current.

1 Using the CAT and the Genny together can give more information than using the CAT alone. Describe how this is done.

2 In the description of the Genny opposite, five methods of applying the signal to buried cables are described. Consider each one in turn and describe:

   a) how they work.

b) what important safety features and precautions are needed.

3 The Genny is also a metal cover locator. How do you think this works?

4 The loudspeaker in the Genny is pointed facing upwards in the induction mode. This will enable the user to hear easily any changes of tone. Describe how the moving coil loudspeaker works.

5 Why do you think it is important to be able to identify exactly all the cables and pipes under the ground. How many types of cables would you expect to find?

6 An alternating signal has a maximum current of 10 A. What is the r.m.s. value of the current if:

   a) it is a sinusoidal signal.

   b) it is a square wave?

   c) What is meant by r.m.s. value?

The Genny applies a distinctive signal. This signal can be applied in five different ways

Induction

The tracing signal is induced on a pipe or cable when the Genny is placed above and in line with the pipe or cable to be located.

Laying the Genny on its side its signal is spread over a wide area induced direct below the Genny.

Always place or hold the Genny at least 5 yards/metres from the C.A.T, otherwise it may pick up signals direct from the Genny instead of from the pipe or cable.

1506 Genny

Battery test
Turn switch to I and listen for bleep signal. Change batteries if there is no sound.

Metal cover location
Remove accessories from storage compartment and equal during control.

Sweeping area holding Genny in normal upright position just above ground will locate large metal covers.

For greater sensitivity for locating valve box covers, sweep area holding Genny horizontally as near as possible to the ground with loudspeaker facing up.
Sharp change in loud-speaker tone indicates presence of metal cover directly below Genny.

Connection
This mode should be used in preference to induction whenever possible

To apply signal connect lead directly to the metal pipe or to the conductor. Connect ground lead to an existing ground point or to a ground stake placed a few yards/metres away and at 90° to the probable line of the buried pipe or cable.

The Genny is a low power and low frequency generator to apply a distinctive pulse signal to buried conductors so that they can be individually selected and traced with the C.A.T. It can also apply its signal over a wide area to buried conductors which can then be located with the C.A.T.

There are five methods of applying the Genny signal to buried conductors.

■ The signal can be connected directly to the conductor. A Connection Lead (1) with alligator clips and a strong magnet are provided for making the connection. A '10 yard Ground Lead on a spool (2) and a Ground Stake (3) are provided for making a ground connection to ensure a strong, easily identified signal flows along the conductor. A distinct change of tone from the loudspeaker indicates that the signal has been successfully applied to the conductor.

■ The Genny signal can be beamed onto a particular buried conductor through up to 3 yards of cover provided the Genny is above the conductor and in line with it. The signal can also be induced onto a conductor by putting the Genny against a street light or against a meter.

■ By laying the Genny on its side in the induction mode its signal spreads over a wide area to all the buried conductors which can then be located with the C.A.T.

■ The Signal Clamp (4), available as an optional extra, applies the Genny signal very selectively to live or dead cables. The cable must have a diameter of 3" or less. The clamp is waterproof and can be used to apply the signal to a cable in a flooded chamber. 28" Extension Rods are available to enable the clamp to be applied to an overhead line

■ The Genny signal can be applied to the wiring system in a building, to the supply line and to the distribution cable by plugging the Plug Connector (5) (optional extra) into a live domestic power socket.

The Genny is also a metal cover locator. Held horizontally just above the ground it registers a sharp change of tone when it is directly above a buried cover. It will locate a 4" valve cover positively at a depth of 6" and a larger cover at depths down to 18"

The Genny is usually unattended during location work. Its yellow stripes are very visible to passers by and its stable shape prevents it being blown over when it is windy. The battery pack is the same as the C.A.T and tone from the loudspeaker indicates that it should be turned off to avoid battery waste when it is no longer required.

Add the Genny to trace and identify

The C.A.T plus the Genny

Together the C.A.T and Genny are a high performance pipe and cable tracer.

The Genny signal can be applied to a metal pipe at a valve or to cables in a sub-station or to any conductor at an accessible point. It applies a distinctive bleep signal to the conductor which is then located and easily recognized using the C.A.T in the **G** mode.

Unenergized street lighting cables and house connections with no **P** or **R** signals can all be traced with the C.A.T once the Genny signal has been applied. Buried conductors indicated by a sweep with the C.A.T in the **P** and **R** search modes can be traced back to a point where their identity can be recognized.

The C.A.T and Genny can also be used together to sweep an area; the Genny signal can be applied to all the buried conductors in a wide area which are then located by the C.A.T.

Summarizing :

■ By itself the C.A.T is a very effective and simple locator with all the advantages of its twin coil system

1 Combination of high sensitivity with a narrow response.

2 Its ability to go on locating and providing information in high interference areas.

3 The additional Radio detection mode for locating unenergized underground conductors.

■ The C.A.T plus Genny combine three different instruments; a super-sensitive cable locator, a classic and selective pipe locator and a lost metal cover locator in a single set of equipment. The three different detection modes in a single set of equipment provides versatility for the user to solve street and highway location problems.

■ Waterproof enclosure for all weather use

■ Rugged sealed monobloc construction for field work.

■ Fast results: combination of automatic gain and manual control makes the equipment simple and speedy to use

■ Designed for the user simple to use with integral instruction panels. Illustrated instruction booklet insures speedy familiarization and user confidence.

MATTER

45 PLAYGROUND PHYSICS

1 If a child of mass 20 kg is on a swing and swings out to a maximum angle of 30° with the vertical, calculate:
    a) the child's maximum gain in potential energy.
    b) the child's maximum kinetic energy.
    c) the child's maximum speed.
    d) the maximum tension in each rope of the swing.
    (Assume the mass of the swing seat and ropes is negligible and the length of the two parallel swing ropes is 3 m.)

2 If Young's modulus for wrought iron is 197 GPa and the ropes of the swing are replaced with rods of wrought iron of the same length but with a cross-section of diameter 1.5 cm (as is seen in some playgrounds), calculate for the same situation as in Question 1:
    a) the maximum stress in the rods.
    b) the maximum strain.
    c) the maximum and minimum extensions during swinging.

3 Discuss how the swinging action is best built up when:
    a) the child is being pushed.
    b) the child is swinging by him/herself.

4 On the roundabout of diameter 4 m, the children can build up a maximum rate of 10 complete turns a minute.
    a) (i) Calculate the centripetal force experienced by a child of mass 35 kg at the maximum speed.
    (ii) Calculate the deceleration of the child as the roundabout comes gradually to a halt from its maximum speed in 3 minutes.
    b) What will happen if a child crawls to the centre of the roundabout while it is in motion?

5 The slide is 3 m high and at an angle of 30° to the horizontal. When it is dry, friction is negligible but when it rains, there is a significant frictional force between the slider and the slide.
    a) Discuss possible reasons for this.
    b) Calculate the final velocity of a 35 kg child when the slide is dry and when the slide is wet, assuming an average frictional force of 10 N in the latter case.

6 Four children want to arrange themselves on the see–saw so that it just balances. The children have masses of 20 kg, 32 kg, 40 kg and 50 kg. Give two examples of arrangements that might be possible if the see–saw is 6 m long.

Read the articles below and overleaf and then answer the questions which follow.

Before launching into the following two reviews, a few notes about the different characteristics of ropes and what some of these numbers mean.

Weight and static strength are pretty obvious. Impact force is a measure of the maximum amount of energy transmitted to the climber during a fall. The lower the number, the less the shock on being pulled up by the rope. The UIAA stipulate a maximum value of 8 kN for one double rope. The figure varies inversely with the stretch value, as a stretchy rope can absorb more energy out of a fall, it also may bounce you down further than you expect and can make jumaring a pain in the bum.

Under UIAA regulations, the maximum stretch allowable for one double rope loaded with 80 kg is 10%. The fall test is conducted on 2.8 m of rope, subjected to a fall factor of 1.78 with a load of 55 kg for a double rope, 80 kg for a single rope. The UIAA stipulates that the rope must survive a minimum of five falls without breakage. It's worth noting here, that older ropes, and ropes which have been subjected to a lot of falls such as in sport climbing, rarely pass this test and often fail on the second, or even, first drop. If you sport climb most weekends, two years may be the maximum life of your rope.

* *

1. Cousin 8.2 mm x 50 m
Supersoft Rope
Weight: 2,335 g
Static Strength: 1,400 kg
Impact Force: 6.1 kN
Stretch for 80 kg: 9.5%
Falls (single rope): 6
Price: £70

Description: This shouldn't be too demanding. A soft feel rope in a rather alarming pink. Also available in a rather alarming yellow.

In Action: As the name says, this is a very soft rope and one which was well liked. Over the summer months, this has been used regularly on Peak Limestone and Welsh mountains and so far is showing little signs of wear. There was no particular problems with kinking despite the rope being frequently used for abseiling. On long pitches, the smooth finish gave noticeably less frictional drag than ropes with a coarser sheath. A slight minus was perhaps the ropes fairly high elasticity but this was never a real problem. The rope market is very competitive, look out for this at special offer price.

For: Performance, low friction.
Against: A little stretchy, colour!
Rating: * * * * *

2. Beal 8.5 mm x 50 m Freestyle Rope
Weight: 2,400 g
Static Strength: 1,450 kg
Impact Force: 5 kN
Stretch for 80 kg: 7.5%
Falls (single rope): 7
Price: £68

Description: Another easy one. A medium/hard feel rope in deep red/pink. Available in various colours and also as a bi-colour.

In Action: Some more gear with nothing much to gripe about. The Freestyle is of a harder construction than the Supersoft, it handled well with no kinking problems despite using it for abseiling. I personally prefer the feel of this slightly harder rope though the only advantage that I can think of is in jumaring where it is less prone to pulling up with the jammer. The coarser sheath also added very slightly to the drag but not so's you notice without using this and the previous ropes together. The Beal was less stretchy than the Supersoft, about right I'd say and the colour was easy on the eyes. A popular rope, again, shop around for the best deals.

For: Performance, good impact force and stretch characteristics.
Against: Nothing really.
Rating: * * * * *

**IMPACT FORCE - ENERGY ABSORPTION
(Rope Dynamic Force)**

The dynamic force of a rope is its ability to absorb the energy generated by a falling climber. To fully understand this phenomenon, we should distinguish between "breaking strength" and the ratio of "impact strength" to rope elongation.

The graph shows three curves representing impact strength relative to elongation and energy absorption for the weight of a climber falling from a height of 2L. This energy is shown as the 'speckled' area.

1) High impact strain/low elongation = hard shock.
2) Low impact strain/high elongation = smooth shock which could be compared to a rubber band.

The ideal situation is shown in the middle curve which balances impact strength and elongation to produce a comfortable, normal shock. The maximum shock (impact force) permitted by the U.I.A.A. is 1200 daN for a single rope and 800 daN for a half rope.

Designed for these major considerations, COUSIN ropes have now become a "must" for climbers. Impact force values are very low thus resulting in excellent energy absorption: below 850 daN (where U.I.A.A. allows up to 1200 daN) and below 600 daN (compared to 800 daN U.I.A.A.).

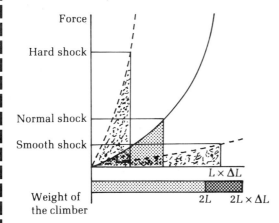

Figure 46.1 Dynamic analysis of a fall (factor 2)

1 Given that the static strength is the maximum force that can be applied to the rope before it snaps:

a) comment on the units used and give a value for the actual maximum force for each rope reviewed.

FACT FILE

Young's modulus = stress/strain
Tensile stress = tension per unit cross–sectional area.
Strain = extension per unit length.
Energy stored per unit volume =
0.5 × stress × strain.
Energy stored =
0.5 × maximum tension × extension.
1 daN = 10 N

b) calculate the maximum stress in each rope before breaking
c) estimate Young's modulus for the material of each rope given that the ropes obey Hooke's Law.

2 The impact force of a rope is a measure of the greatest force that can be exerted on the climber during a fall. Explain what you understand by this statement and discuss why the article says the impact force is a measure of energy transmitted to the climber during a fall. Why is the shock less on being pulled up by the rope if the impact force is less?

3 A fall factor is defined as the length of fall divided by the amount of rope in a belay system. Why can a fall factor not be greater than 2?

4 a) Using energy considerations calculate the amount by which a Beal rope would stretch if a climber of mass 60 kg fell a distance of 5 m before the rope was straight given a belay of 10m.
b) Calculate the maximum tensions for a fall factor of 2 in the Cousins rope and the Beal rope, assuming that Hooke's law holds throughout.

5 Compare your answers in Question 4b) with the impact forces quoted. Explain any discrepancies with reference to the graph shown. What should the graphs look like if Hooke's law applied? Comment on the axis label $L \times \Delta L$.

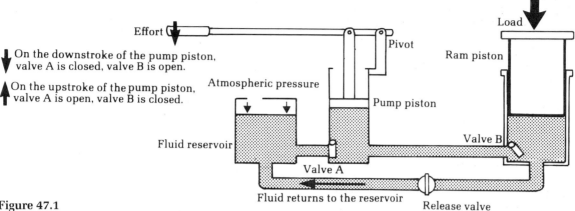

Figure 47.1

The transmission of pressure through incompressible liquids means that the heaviest of objects can be easily lifted using hydraulic lifts. It means that cars can be braked safely without having to apply an enormous force. The applications of this principle are all around you - see how many you can observe in one day.

*F*ACT FILE

Work done = force × distance moved in the direction of the force.
Pressure = force/area.
Efficiency = output/input.

1 Locks work to enable craft to move up or down a canal when there is a difference in water level between two sections.
a) Describe how the boat is lifted upstream when the lock is in operation.
b) Where does the energy come from to lift the boat?

2 What examples in the area of animal physiology can you find showing the use of hydraulic pressure?

3 a) Find out how hydraulic brakes work.
b) Why is it extremely dangerous if an air leak gets into the hydraulic braking system?

4 A hydraulic jack applies a force to just lift a car of mass 1000 kg. If the ratio of the area of the platform for the car to the plunger on the jack is 20:1, calculate:
a) the force exerted on the plunger.
b) the total distance moved down by the plunger if the car is raised by one metre.
c) What will cause an efficiency of less than 100 ?

5 a) In Alsace, there is a giant lock that lifts the boats through a height of about 35 m. If a cruiser has a mass of about 1500 kg, calculate:
(i) the work done on the boat lifting it to this new level.
(ii) the energy stored in the water column when the lock is full. Assume the lock shaft has a cross–sectional area of 200 m². (Density of water = 1000 kg m⁻³.)
(iii) the energy of the water released down stream after the double cycle of one boat being taken upstream and another boat being taken down stream.
b) How could the energy in a) (iii) be used in some productive fashion?

ROCK AND ROLLING MILLS: THE SIGNS IN THE STONES

Metallurgists study how to process a metal or alloy to influence its crystal structure and physical properties. Geologists do the opposite: they take a deformed rock, and find out how it formed. In the 1970s, geologists realised that ideas from materials science could tell them whether rocks had come to their final shapes at high or low temperatures, quickly or slowly, or in wet or dry conditions. A simple example comes from two methods of steel production - hot working and cold working. Each leaves behind distinct imperfections in the crystals of the metal.

Cold working consists of rolling steel at relatively low temperatures. Individual crystals distort to take up the strain as the sheet becomes thinner. Planes of atoms in the crystals slide past each other, breaking and reforming bonds between individual atoms. The pattern of bonds alters to form linear breaks called dislocations in the otherwise regular structure.

As the rolling continues to stress the crystal lattice, bonds between atoms break and reform and the dislocations move, on different planes within the lattice. When two or more dislocations that are moving through the lattice intersect, they become tangled up, and neither can move farther. Sometimes dislocations moving on the same plane pile up; otherwise the tangles localise where two lattice planes intersect. As a result, the steel becomes harder as it is worked.

Hot working has a different effect. At higher temperatures dislocations form and move through the lattice, but they do not tangle up. Because the steel is warmer, atoms in the lattice have more energy, and bonds can move in different ways to relieve the local stresses around a dislocation. In particular, bonds can break and reform all around the defects, so that dislocations are no longer restricted to their own planes. They can continue to move without tangling, and the steel can reach much higher strains

without hardening.

Metals worked in these ways look very different under a transmission electron microscope (TEM). Cold worked steel has dense areas of tangled dislocations throughout the crystals. Hot working leaves many areas of the crystal with few dislocations; what defects there are form the edges of these subgrains. These areas have not been completely protected from distortion. They have been distorted, and have subsequently recovered; this is why hot working can achieve higher strain.

Geologists find these two types of deformation interesting for two reasons. First, they can tell them apart; secondly, they represent relatively cool and hot deformation. Likewise, other deformation mechanisms produce distinguishing features that might indicate high stress, or fluid pressure or even the strain rate. These microstructures revealed the processes that deformed rocks such as mylonites. Mylonites are tough, banded, finegrained rocks that geologists had associated with fault zones for more than a hundred years. The microstructures of these rocks resembles textures of hot-rolled steel, especially in TEM. Mylonites are clearly products of a hot working process, at relatively high temperatures. Lower temperature deformation could crush and grind down rocks into fragments, but without the same dislocation structures.

So began the search for different mechanisms of deformation, and the physical conditions they represented. Geologists realised they could produce some textures that matched real rocks in a matter of a few months. But how could experiments hope to reproduce millions of years of infinitesimally slow geological deformation? One way was to concentrate on the speedier aspects of deformation - fracturing and crushing. Another was to choose softer rocks such as limestone, or to run experiments at higher temperatures.

Experimenters try to use relatively simple rocks such as pure quartzites, limestones, and granite with uniform grain sizes. They mount small cylinders a few centimetres high in presses and surround them with fluid under pressure to mimic the pressure underground from surrounding rocks. The results have helped quantify the processes behind some common features of naturally deformed rocks.

One important mechanism, albeit very slow, is diffusional mass transfer, in which minerals dissolve at some places and precipitate elsewhere, changing the overall shape of the rock. This process makes ice skating possible: ice, like minerals such as calcite, is more soluble when compressed. Beneath the blade of a skate, ice melts to make a slippery film of water, on which you glide. Once the pressure drops, the water freezes back into ice. In rocks, grains tend to dissolve fastest in the direction of the greatest compression. The effect is especially important in limestone and dolomite; it often happens at different rates through the rock, because of impurities and variations in crystal structure. Cataclasis (fracturing) is also important, especially in the top ten kilometres or so of the Earth's crust. Fractured rocks are often permeable also; this can speed up further fracture, by bringing chemicals such as water that weaken the rock to the vulnerable tips of cracks. It also contributes to faster weathering of fault zones, which often form valleys.

F_ACT FILE

Young's modulus = stress/strain.
Tensile stress = tension per unit cross–sectional area.
Strain = extension per unit length.

1 Explain in terms of the crystal lattice and dislocations why hot working of steel enables it to reach much higher strains without hardening.

2 a) Why do geologists find the crystal structure of hot and cold worked steel particularly interesting?
b) Why is grain size important?

3 a) What piece of equipment was essential to this piece of research?
b) Describe the experiments that have helped to quantify what has happened in the past to some types of rock.

c) The scientists have recognised that three mechanisms are important in the shaping of our rocky landscapes, crushing, diffusional mass transfer and fracturing. What effects does each of these processes produce?

4 Why is ice skating possible?

5 A typical rock has an axial modulus of 3×10^{11} Pa where

$$\text{the axial modulus} = \frac{\text{compressional stress}}{\text{compressional strain}}.$$

Given that the average density of earth materials is 5500 kg m^{-3}, calculate:
a) the compressional stress on rocks at the bottom of Scafell Pike directly under the summit (height 1000 m).
b) the compressional strain.

Hot air balloooning is a fast growing sport giving a sense of peace and timelessness to the participants. The burners have to be operated intermittently in all parts of a flight. Hydrogen–filled balloons have also been used for flights as have helium–filled balloons. The main problem with hydrogen balloons is the risk of fire. This was seen in the disastrous loss of the hydrogen–filled airship the R101 in 1930.

Fact File

Archimedes' principle states that the upthrust of a fluid on an immersed solid is equal to the weight of the fluid displaced.

A floating body displaces its own weight of fluid.

For a fixed mass of gas $\dfrac{P_1 V_1}{T_1} = \dfrac{P_2 V_2}{T_2}$ where

P = the pressure, V = the volume and T = the temperature in K.

$P = \dfrac{1}{3}\rho c^2$ where ρ = the density and

c^2 = the mean square speed of the gas molecules.

1 a) Explain why any balloon will eventually stop rising.
b) Why are weather balloons designed to eventually burst.
c) Why does the burner have to be used in the hot–air balloon:
    (i) when it is rising?
    (ii) when it is maintaining steady flight?
    (iii) when it is coming down?

2 Helium replaced hydrogen in airships because of the fire hazard. An airship has a volume of 10 000 m³. How much weight will it lift, in addition to its own, when filled with:
a) hydrogen?
b) helium?
(Density of hydrogen = 0.09 kg m⁻³, density of helium = 0.18 kg m⁻³, density of air = 1.3 kg m⁻³.)

3 An advertising helium–filled balloon is tethered at ground level. If the volume of the balloon is 20 m³ and the mass of the material of the balloon excluding the gas is 10 kg, calculate the force on the mooring point if no wind is blowing.
(Assume the mass of the rope is negligible compared to the mass of the balloon.)

4 A hot–air balloon has a volume of 500 m³ and the density of the surrounding air is 1.2 kg m⁻³. If the balloon is hovering and the burner has heated the air inside until it has a density of 0.75 kg m⁻³, calculate:
a) the total mass of the balloon material and the load.
b) the net upward force on the balloon if the density of the air inside is further reduced to 0.70 kg m⁻³.
c) the acceleration with which the balloon will now rise.

5 A balloon has a volume of 1000 m³ at ground level when filled with hydrogen at a density of 0.09 kg m⁻³.

a) What is the mass of the hydrogen used?

b) What will be the new volume of the balloon at 1000 m if the pressure is now reduced from 100 kPa at ground level to 88 kPa at the new height?

(You can assume the material of the balloon is such that it does not restrict the change in volume.)

c) What will be the new density of the hydrogen in the balloon?

d) How much weight can the balloon carry, in addition to its own, if it is just going to rise to a height of 1000 m where the density of air is 1.1 kg m⁻³?

6 In Question 5 the situation is actually more complex as the air temperature falls with increasing height. If the air temperature falls by 8 °C and the temperature at ground level is 15 °C, calculate the effect that this will have on your answers to Question 5 a), b), c) and d).

7 a) Calculate the root mean square velocity of oxygen molecules in air:

(i) at a pressure of 100 kPa and a density of 1.3 kg m⁻³.

(ii) at a pressure of 88 kPa and a density of 1.1 kg m⁻³.

b) Why does the atmosphere have a particular height or thickness?

50 ▶ THERMOMETERS

Read the article below and then answer the questions which follow.

Taking the temperature

Thermometer design has come a long way since the first known thermometer was made by Galileo in around 1600. This consisted of a glass bulb containing air with an open-ended tube. The whole apparatus was inverted so that the tube dipped into a beaker of water. The height the water rose up the tube was affected by the temperature of the air in the bulb. Unfortunately this was not the only thing that affected the height of the water. In addition, the thermometer had no fixed points and so was not accurate. A replica of an alternative design by Galileo is shown in the photogragh. This was more accurate but still had no fixed points to establish the scale.

The first sealed thermometer was made by Ferdinand, Duke of Tuscany, in 1694. However, scientists didn't realise the importance of using a temperature scale with two fixed points until Sir Isaac Newton pointed this out in 1701. The fixed points suggested by Newton were the freezing point of water, to be called 0°, and the temperature of the human body, to be called 12°.

In 1713, Fahrenheit made a thermometer calling the lowest temperature that he could achieve with a salt and ice mixture 0°, and the temperature of the human body 12°. He then divided each degree into eight so body temperature became 96° and on this scale the freezing point of water was 32° and the boiling point 212°.

In 1742, Celsius used the fixed points of freezing and boiling water under standard pressure conditions to create the Celsius scale used today.

Scientists today use a constant volume gas thermometer as a standard against which all other thermometers are calibrated. The ideal gas scale has two fixed points - absolute zero and the triple point of water.

Many kinds of thermometers are used today to cater for wide-ranging conditions. The strip thermometer which is used to give a quick indication of a child's temperature is just one of the many recent developments in the science of thermometry.

FACT FILE

$\theta/°C = T/K - 273.15$

$$t_m = \frac{(X_m - X_l)}{X_u - X_l} N + t_l$$

1 a) Why was Galileo's first thermometer inaccurate?
b) Describe how you think the replica design works. Why is it important to have the weights very accurately made?

2 Until recently both Fahrenheit and Celsius thermometers have been in common use.
a) "The temperature in the south will be up in the 80s today" refers to which scale? What is the equivalent value on the other scale?
b) "Your normal body temperature is 98.4°" refers to which scale? What is the equivalent value on the other scale?

3 Two equations are given in the Fact file. What do they refer to and how are they useful?

4 a) Why do scientists use the constant volume gas thermometer as the standard thermometer and why isn't it in common use?
b) What is meant by the triple point for water?

5 The article has failed to mention one emminent scientist, Kelvin, who worked in this field. Why is his work important?

6 A resistance thermometer has a resistance of 40.4 Ω when measuring an unknown temperature. Its resistance is 38.1 Ω when immersed in melting ice, and 41.0 Ω when held in steam above boiling water at standard pressure.
a) Calculate the unknown temperature on the Celsius scale of the resistance thermometer.
b) Would this necessarily agree exactly with the reading taken by a different type of thermometer still using a Celsius scale?

7 a) Give an account of the different thermometers in use today along with reasons for using them under different conditions and temperature ranges.
b) Find out how a strip thermometer works.

Quick action saves sight

When driving in the mountains a common problem is overheated cooling systems. On investigating such overheating while driving in snow, a faulty radiator cap caused a jet of steam and boiling water to hit Mr. James full in the face. His wife quickly collected snow from the verge and packed it onto his face. She kept snow on his skin for as long as he could stand it. The result was no damage to his eyes and only two small blisters on his forehead. Mr. James believes that quick reflex action stopped a direct hit into his eyes and that the snow reduced the temperature so quickly that severe burning was completely stopped. 'I felt like food being cooled for the freezer.' he joked with our reporter.

FIRST AID

Burns and scalds can cause serious disabilities, your prompt and correct action in an emergency could reduce suffering.
The Emergency Aid for burns is based on the simple fact that heat does the damage and so you must immediately cool down the affected area.
The best Emergency Aid for a minor accident is to hold the burn under cold water (or any other cold, harmless liquid) for at least 10 minutes.
The general Emergency Aid for burns is therefore based on common-sense - you use cold water to cool the skin.

FACT FILE

$\Delta Q = mc\Delta\theta$ where ΔQ = the heat supplied to a body, m = the mass of the body, c = the specific heat capacity, and $\Delta\theta$ = the temperature rise.
$\Delta Q = ml$ where ΔQ = the heat supplied to a solid or liquid, m = the mass of the solid or liquid that changes state and l = the specific latent heat of fusion or vaporisation.

1 a) By what processes was the skin being cooled and why was speed so important in the first aid given above?
b) What initial quick reflex reactions would stop a direct hit on the eyes?

2 Why did the snow need renewing?

3 Why is a scald from steam at 100 °C more severe than a scald from water at 100 °C?

4 When cooking and freezing food, it is important to cool hot food quickly before putting it in the freezer. Suppose 250 g of stew is at 80 °C and is surrounded by 500 g of water at 10 °C.
a) Estimate the final temperature of the stew.
b) State what assumptions you have made.
c) What is the main reason for cooling the food quickly?
(Assume the average specific heat capacity of stew is 3000 J kg^{-1} °C^{-1} and the specific heat capacity of water is 4200 J kg^{-1} °C^{-1}.)

5 Suppose the same mass of stew as in Question 3 was surrounded by 500 g of crushed ice at 0 °C, the stew was left until a temperature of 0 °C was reached and the stew was still **not** frozen.
a) What would happen to the ice?
b) Estimate the proportion of the ice that melts.
c) State what assumptions you have made.
(the specific latent heat of fusion of ice is 340 000 J kg^{-1}.)

6 a) In Questions 3 and 4, how much heat was removed from the beef stew?
b) Why would it **not** be a good idea to keep ice on a skin burn for too long?
c) The first aid manual recommends holding minor burns under cold running water. Why is this preferable to the snow treatment?

If a kettle, iron or central heating system gets coated with scale in an area where the drinking water is alkaline, the deposits formed can affect the heat flow and the efficiency of the system.

*F*ACT FILE

$\frac{Q}{t} = \frac{kA(\theta_1 - \theta_2)}{L}$ where Q/t = the rate of flow of heat, k = the thermal conductivity, A = the cross–sectional area, $(\theta_1 - \theta_2)$ = the temperature difference and L = the conductor length.

1 Given that the drinking water is alkaline in areas where scale is a problem:
   a) what do you think scale deposits may consist of?
   b) what might the descaler fluid be?
   c) why is the container's child safety cap important?

2 What are the main problems if scale gets into a central heating system and how are they overcome?

3 The base of a stainless steel kettle designed to go on a gas or electric hob is 2.5 mm thick and has a diameter of 20 cm. If the base of the pan is covered with a layer of scale 1.0 mm thick, calculate:
   a) the temperature of the bottom of the pan when the water is boiling and the rate of heat flow into the pan is 3 kW.
   b) the temperature of the bottom of the pan with the same heat flow if the pan has been descaled.
   (k for stainless steel = 150 Wm^{-1} K^{-1} and k for scale = 1.0 Wm^{-1} K^{-1}.)

c) Why will the scale affect the time the kettle takes to boil?

4 Sketch a graph to show how the temperature varies with distance across the thickness of the base of the pan in Question 3 when the water is boiling and:
   a) the scale is present.
   b) the scale has been removed.

5 **a)** What effect would a thin layer of dirt have on the outside of the base of the kettle?
   b) Check your ideas with a calculation assuming that the thermal conductivity of dirt is 0.001 times that of stainless steel, that there is a layer of dirt 0.1 mm thick and that there is no scale inside the pan.

53 ► INSULATION

GRANTS TO HELP INSULATE YOUR LOFT - SAVE ENERGY!

USE CAVITY WALL INSULATION - AND KEEP WARM

DOUBLE GLAZING SAVES YOU MONEY

SOLAR VILLAGES PLANNED FOR LADAKH

The Indian government has promised to help pay for the introduction of solar technology on a large scale in the region of Ladakh, just south of Tibet. The plan is to build 100 solar "walls" and 100 greenhouses a year, which will make Ladakh one of the most prominent regions in the world for solar energy.

At an international conference held last week in Leh, the capital of Ladakh, the District Development Commissioner for the region, S.S. Kapur, said that the government intends to subsidise by 75 per cent the cost of special solar walls in houses and greenhouses.

Ladakh is probably the most suitable place in the world for exploiting solar energy. Most of the country is above 3000 metres, the average rainfall is less than 10 centimetres a year, and cloud cover is minimal. Clear skies and intense sunlight all year round make sophisticated solar systems unnecessary.

The solar "walls", for instance, are quite simple in design: the south-facing wall of brick is painted black for maximum absorption of sunlight. The wall is made with air vents at the top and bottom and is double glazed. The distance between the wall and the glass is generally about eight centimetres.

Light absorbed by the black surface heats the wall and is re-radiated as longer wavelengths. Light at these wavelengths cannot penetrate the glass and so is trapped within the airspace. The air between the wall and the glass is heated and enters the inside of the room by the upper air vent. Cooler air then comes in through the lower vent to replace this air.

At night, the wall continues to radiate stored heat into the room. The plan is to introduce such walls into the homes of Ladakh's 254 villages. The solar walls pay for themselves within two years.

The solar greenhouses are similar in design. This time, two large oil drums, one containing water and the other containing antifreeze, radiate heat during the night and help to keep temperatures high enough to grow vegetables during the winter. This has the effect of expanding the short growing season of June to September by allowing families to grow seedlings that are then ready to plant at the very beginning of the season.

Given the world problems of energy supplies conserving energy becomes more and more important. New houses are constantly being designed to have greater energy saving properties and to use renewable energy supplies.

Read the article above carefully and then answer the questions which follow.

F*ACT FILE*

The thermal resistance coefficient of a material is the thermal resistance per unit area of the material. For material of thermal conductivity k and thickness L, the thermal resistance coefficient = L/k.

Different surfaces and cavities also have equivalent thermal resistance coefficients.

The U value of a wall or window is the heat flow per square metre of surface produced by a temperature difference of 1 K. The U value is the reciprocal of the total thermal resistance coefficient for the item.

1 Describe the way the solar walls work in Ladakh with particular attention to the ways that heat energy is being transferred.

2 How do the solar greenhouses work? Why do you need two drums?

3 In how many ways do we conserve heat energy in our houses today?

4 a) From the information in the fact file deduce the units for:
    (i) the thermal resistance coefficient.
    (ii) the U value.
b) Show that for a composite wall made of several layers with different U factors that

$$\frac{1}{U} = \frac{1}{U_1} + \frac{1}{U_2} + \frac{1}{U_3}$$ where U is the value for

the composite item and U_1, U_2, U_3 are the values for the surfaces, layers and cavities that make up the whole.

5 a) Calculate the total thermal resistance coefficient and the U value of a cavity–filled wall given that the inner and outer surface thermal resistance coefficients of the wall are 0.05 and 0.14 respectively, that the thermal resistance coefficient of the cavity filling is 0.25, that the thickness of each brick wall is 30 cm and that the thermal conductivity of brick is 0.4 W m^{-1}K^{-1}.

b) What is the total heat flow through such a house wall of area 100 m^2 if the temperature difference between the inside and the outside is 10 °C?
c) How would your results in a) and b) differ if the wall was just made of a layer of single brick?

6 a) Calculate the total thermal resistance coefficient and the U value of a double–glazed window given that the inner and outer surface thermal resistance coefficients of the glass are 0.05 and 0.14 respectively, that the thermal resistance coefficient of the cavity is 0.15, that the thickness of each glass pane is 5 mm and that the thermal conductivity of glass is 1.0 W m^{-1} K^{-1}.
b) What is the total heat flow through a window of area 1.0 m^2 if the temperature difference between the inside and the outside is 10 °C?
c) How would your results in a) and b) differ if the window was just made of a single glass pane?

7 Estimate the relative value to a consumer of double glazing or cavity wall filling. What else will you need to find out?

54   USING A MICROWAVE OVEN

Microwaves are electromagnetic waves which are produced by a device called a magnetron. The waves are reflected by metal and penetrate food to a depth of about 4 cm. Any substance which contains water, fat or sugar is rapidly heated by the waves.

Look at the brochure on the opposite page and then answer the questions which follow.

FACT FILE

$\Delta Q = mc\Delta\theta$ where ΔQ = the heat supplied to a body, m = the mass of the body, c = the specific heat capacity, and $\Delta\theta$ = the temperature rise.
$\Delta Q = ml$ where ΔQ = the heat supplied to a solid or liquid, m = the mass of the solid or liquid that changes state and l = the specific latent heat of fusion or vaporisation.

M I C R O W A V E   O V E N

NN 6850 White

NN 6800 Brown

(This model includes an oven lamp)

The *Genius* is the top of the family size range of microwave ovens.

The 9 *Auto Programs* clearly displayed on the panel use the humidity sensor. This sensor detects the steam given off from the food as it begins to cook and calculates the remaining cooking time for you.

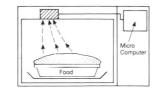

Micro Computer

Food

The *Auto Reheat* pad automatically reheats home plated meals, again using the humidity sensor.

Defrosting frozen foods couldn't be easier – the *Auto Defrost* feature selects the correct defrosting time required, once you have told the oven the type of food and weight.

In addition to the *Genius* automatic features, this oven offers manual cooking with *6 Power Settings* to choose from 90-800 Watts (IEC).

1 All microwave ovens have the microwaves reflecting off the insides of the cavity in a pattern determined by cavity dimensions.

a) How do different makes of oven tackle the problems of localised cold spots?

b) How can you establish where cold spots are in a particular oven and adapt your cooking techniques accordingly?

c) Why is this important from a health point of view?

2 The magnetron in a particular microwave has only one power output. Discuss and explain how different settings are achieved for cooking.

3 **a)** It is not a good idea to switch on a microwave oven without food or water in the oven and metal containers or china plates with metallic decoration should never be used. Explain why.

b) Sometimes cooking instructions recommend using small pieces of foil to protect thin portions of food such as a fish tail. However a warning is usually given that the heating pattern in the oven may alter when this is done. Explain what is happening.

4 Microwave ovens should be checked for leaks and have three switches for operation to ensure that they can never be on when the door is open. Why do you think this is necessary? Discuss.

5 **a)** Larger items such as joints of meat often have cooking instructions which state that after cooking in the microwave they must be wrapped in metallic foil and left for ten minutes or so to finish cooking. What is happening?

b) A cylindrical joint has a mass of 1.5 kg a diameter of 10 cm and is 20 cm in length. If after cooking the outside layer of 3 cm thickness is at a temperature of 100 °C, estimate the equilibrium temperature after the meat has been kept in foil after cooking. (Assume the centre portion of the joint is still at a room temperature of 18 °C immediately after cooking.)

c) We have been using an extremely simplified model of the situation in part b). How is the situation more complex?

6 Some microwave ovens incorporate humidity sensors. Information on the type of food being cooked also has to be put into the automatic programme. Discuss why this is necessary and how the inputs will be used. A flow diagram may help here.

Are we at risk?

In Britain we each receive, on average, a dose of radiation giving energy absorbed by the body tissue of 2.2×10^{-3} J kg^{-1}. Of this, 87% is due to naturally occuring background radiation. An example contributing to a small part of this is the emission of radon gas from naturally occuring uranium in rocks. To put the average dose into context, a lethal dose would be 10 J kg^{-1}. Interestingly, if a major catastrophe caused the level of background radiation to rise dramatically, insects would have a far greater chance of survival than animals. An insect can survive a dose in excess of 100 J kg^{-1}.

The harm is done through the ionisation caused by the radiation. The ions produced in body tissue can damage the DNA molecules in the nuclei of body cells. This can lead to the activation of cancer–causing genes and other problems. Different types of radiation have different ionisation effects. α–particles have greater ionisation densities per metre of path than β particles which in turn have greater ionisation densities than γ–rays.

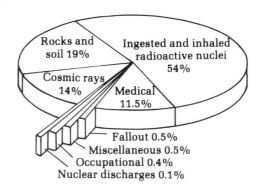

Figure 55.1 Approximate contributions to the dose of ionising radiation received on average by people living in the UK

Given the low annual dose rate there would seem to be little risk to human health but scientists are continually monitoring the effects of radiation and with accidents such as Chernobyl there is no room for complacency.

$\mathbf{F}$ACT FILE

The penetration range of each type of ionising radiation in the body is very different. It varies from 10^{-5} to 10^{-4} m for α–particles, 10^{-3} to 10^{-2} m for β–particles and right through the body for γ–rays.
$E = hf$

1 **a)** What are the main sources of naturally–occuring background radiation?
   b) Why has radon gas been isolated recently as a particular problem in places such as Cornwall?

2 The article mentions other problems in connection with the damage to DNA. What do you think these might be?

3 **a)** Which type of ionising radiation will have the greatest effect on body tissue? Explain.
   b) Safety precautions differ when working with materials which produce α–particles and working with γ–rays. What do you think the differences will be and why?

4 The pie chart compares average doses of received radiation.
   a) Why will this vary from one part of the country to another?
   b) Why will this vary from one individual to another?
   c) What precautions can an individual take?
   d) Why do people who work at high altitudes have a greater background dosage?

5 As a result of the potential hazards, strict precautions are needed when working with radioactive materials. Find out about and list precautions that are taken when working:
a) with closed sources in schools.
b) in the nuclear industry and in hospitals.

6 Why should γ–rays cause some ionisation within body tissue but infrared radiation does not? Support your answer with a calculation.

7 Find out about the accident at the nuclear power station at Chernobyl. How can such accidents be prevented in the future?

56 RADIOACTIVE DATING

Read the article below and then answer the questions which follow.

The age of once living material like this fossilised tree can be found by using radiocarbon dating. The carbon content of living materials consists of the radioisotope carbon-14 and the stable isotope carbon-12. The relative proportions of these two isotopes in the atmosphere, and hence in living things, can be assumed to have remained constant over long periods of time. This is because carbon–14 is continually being produced at a constant rate by the action of cosmic rays on the upper atmosphere and is also decaying at a constant rate.

However when a living organism dies it is no longer taking in carbon-14 and the existing carbon-14 in the body will start to decrease as radioactive decay proceeds. By comparing amounts of carbon-14 in fossilised plants and living plants it is possible to establish the age of the fossil.

The age of rocks, which involves relatively long time scales, is established by looking at the relative amounts of a parent and daughter isotope in a particular sample. From this, the age of the rock can be calculated provided none of the daughter isotope was present when the rock first solidified and none has been lost since.

Parent isotope	Daughter isotope	Half-life
$^{14}_{6}\text{C}$	$^{14}_{7}\text{N}$	5730a
$^{235}_{92}\text{U}$	$^{207}_{82}\text{Pb}$	704Ma
$^{238}_{92}\text{U}$	$^{206}_{82}\text{Pb}$	4467Ma
$^{87}_{37}\text{Rb}$	$^{87}_{38}\text{Sr}$	48800Ma

Decay constant $\lambda = \frac{\ln 2}{T\frac{1}{2}}$ and $N = N_o e^{-\lambda t}$ where

$T\frac{1}{2}$ = the half–life, N = the number of radio-active atoms remaining at time t, N_o = the number present initially.

1 Suppose you have a sample of rock that you suspect is about 1000 Ma (million years) old. Which isotope would you hope to find and use to date your sample?

2 Why is radioactive carbon-14 not used for establishing geological time scales?

3 Write down the full equation for the decay of carbon-14 and explain the process in the nucleus that has given rise to this reaction.

4 The age of the Dead Sea scrolls was measured using radio–carbon dating. If the measurements gave a ratio of 0.78 for the ratio of the activity in the sample to the activity in a sample of corresponding live material of similar mass, calculate the age of the scrolls.

5 A sample of wood taken from an Egyptian tomb was found to have a count rate of 8.4 counts per minute per gram of carbon. A sample of living wood has a count rate of 15.2 counts per minute per gram of carbon. Estimate the age of the tomb.

6 a) How many half lives have passed since a particular rock was formed if a sample of the rock contains 31 times as much lead–207 than uranium–235?
b) How old is the rock and what have you assumed in your reasoning?

7 If a rock has a parent:daughter isotope ratio of 1:10 and the parent isotope is Rb–87 calculate the age of the rock sample.

8 The half–life of lead–210 is 22 years. Commercial lead contains minute amounts of this isotope. Why do you think physicists are interested in using lead from old cannon balls to shield delicate radioactive experiments?

57 SMOKE DETECTORS

Read the article on the opposite page and then answer the questions which follow.

FACT FILE

Electronic charge = 1.60×10^{-19} C

$N = N_o e^{-\lambda t}$; $\lambda = \frac{\ln 2}{T\frac{1}{2}}$; Activity = $\frac{-dN}{dt} = \lambda N$

1 Why is it likely that the source inside an ionisation detector is an α-emitter?

2 Why must the source be sealed?

3 'It is also considered safe to dispose of ionisation detectors eventually in normal household refuse.' What does this statement imply about the radioactive source used ?

4 If a source has an activity of 1500 particles emitted per second and the average number of ion pairs created by a single α-particle is 5.2×10^4 calculate the maximum ionisation current in the smoke detector.

5 A sample of radioactive material in an alarm contains 10^{12} atoms. The half–life of the material is 4 years. Calculate:
    a) the initial activity.

b) the fraction of undecayed atoms remaining after 1 year.
c) the activity of the sample after 1 year.
d) the maximum possible ionisation current after 1 year.

6 Hopefully the currents you have calculated are rather small!
    a) How are they *reduced* in size by a fire?
    b) How can such a reduction in the current be used to trigger a smoke alarm buzzer which will need a much bigger current flowing through it?

c) Design a possible circuit to trigger the alarm buzzer.
d) How might an override button of the type described be incorporated into the circuit you have designed ?

7 Why do you think a photoelectric detector might be more sensitive to smoke from slowly smouldering fires?

8 Design a circuit for a smoke alarm using a photoelectric device rather than a radioactive source. Explain how your circuit and the photoelectric device work.

FAMILY SAVED BY SMOKE ALARM

Smouldering wiring in a loft nearly caused a major tragedy in Almsdale Road, West Underthorpe. The fire that developed in the middle of the night was detected by a new smoke alarm that the owners of the house, Mr and Mrs Baxter, had only installed one week earlier.

"The firemen tell me that the smoke alarm saved us from being suffocated by the fumes in our sleep" said a relieved and grateful Mr Baxter.

It also appears that the early warning prevented much more damage being done by the developing flames.

Our readers may like to consider the following information about smoke alarms which are strongly recommended by the fire brigade.

Smoke alarms are easy to install and give a loud signal and a flashing light when smoke is detected. The commonest type is the ionisation smoke alarm. This detector is particularly good at detecting hot blazing fires. The detector has a small radioactive source inside which ionises the air close to it. The ions produced are charged and allow a weak current to flow from a battery. The presence of smoke particles changes the current flow and sets off the alarm. The radioactive source presents no hazard to health as it is sealed and very weak. If the

detector wears out it can easily be disposed of with normal household rubbish but it is important to make sure the sealed source is not broken.

Another type of smoke detector contains a photo-electric device which detects a light beam. If the light intensity is reduced by smoke the alarm goes off. This type of detector is very good at detecting slowly smouldering fires.

58 ► FLUORESCENT LAMPS

Lightbulbs have come a long way since the first discharge tubes were invented by William Crookes in 1870. He passed an electric discharge through gases at low pressure and found that the colour of the discharge seen depended on the gas in the tube. Such discharges gave rise to line spectra when the light was passed through a diffraction grating or a prism.

The first street fluorescent lamps used either mercury vapour which gave a bluish light or sodium lamps which gave a yellow light. The latter had the advantage that they produced improved illumination in fog but had the disadvantage that all colours except yellow looked different shades of grey. This produced amazing effects. People walking home at night looked terrible. It really wasn't acceptable and modern fluorescent lights have coatings inside which absorb some of the initial radiation from the gas in the lamp and reradiate it at different frequencies to give a light closer to the continuous spectrum from the Sun.

Now compact fluorescent lamps are being used instead of ordinary lightbulbs in the home with energy saving advantages.

FACT FILE

$E_2 - E_1 = hf$ where E_2 and E_1 are electron energy levels in an atom and hf = the energy of the emitted photon.
$h = 6.63 \times 10^{-34}$ Js
$c = 3.00 \times 10^8$ ms^{-1}
1 eV $= 1.60 \times 10^{-19}$ J

1 Describe how the characteristic colours arise in the excited gases in the discharge tubes and why they give rise to line spectra.

2 Why did the early sodium lamps give such peculiar lighting?

WOTAN DELUX BULBS

| Brightness 11W | Power consumption 20% | Lamp life 8000h |

Not dimmable **11W** 240 -250V 50/60 Hz

3 Why were the lamps good fog lamps rather than ordinary lights?

4 Describe how the coatings worked in terms of energy levels and excitation.

5 The wavelengths of visible light emitted from a hydrogen lamp are 656 nm, 486 nm, 434 nm and 410 nm.
   a) What photon energies do these correspond to?
   b) If they are all due to electron jumps down to the second energy level in the hydrogen atom at 10.2 eV, calculate the next four energy levels in eV.

6 a) Calculate the energy in eV of photons of sodium light of wavelength 590 nm.
   b) If the distance travelled by electrons in the sodium lamp between collisions is 1.0×10^{-4} m, calculate the electric field strength needed to cause the emission of the sodium light.
   c) What would happen to the electric field strength needed if the gas was at a higher pressure?

7 a) How much energy would be saved in a week if the modern lightbulb shown was on for 4 hr every night instead of an ordinary bulb giving the same illumination.
   b) Why does this bulb have such a low power consumption compared to an ordinary bulb?

59 RADIATION PRESSURE FROM THE SUN

Radiation pressure at the Earth's surface due to radiation from the Sun can be measured. It is however very small, about 10^{-6} Pa.

FACT FILE

$E = hf$ and $p = h/\lambda$ where E = the energy of a photon, p = the momentum, h = Planck constant = 6.63×10^{-34} J s, f = the frequency of the electromagnetic radiation and λ = the wavelength.

1 a) Using the information in the Fact file write down an expression for the change of momentum when a photon of light from the Sun strikes a surface normally and is:
   (i) absorbed.
   (ii) reflected.
   b) What is the impulse given to the surface in the case of a)(i) and (ii)?

2 What is the total change of momentum per second per square metre of surface in each case in Question 1 if n = the number of photons per second per square metre which strike the surface normally?

3 a) By considering Newton's second law, write down an expression for the pressure at a surface when photons strike the surface normally and are:
   (i) absorbed.
   (ii) reflected.
   b) Carry out a units check to see if your expressions in a)(i) and (ii) have the correct units for pressure.

4 How would the pressure on the surface be changed if the photons were reflected as before but were incident at an angle of 60° to the normal?

5 A sodium lamp emits light of wavelength 590 nm. If the lamp has an emissive power of 60 W and emits the light isotropically, calculate:
   a) the total number of photons emitted per second.
   b) the number of photons incident per second per square metre at a distance of 0.5 m.
   c) the pressure due to the photons from the lamp if incident normally on on a reflective surface at a distance of 0.5 m from the lamp.

6 The above analysis that you have carried out assumes the particle model for light. When is it appropriate to use the particle model and when should you use the wave model?

7 What would happen to the magnitude of the radiation pressure from the Sun if the distance to the Sun was halved?

Read the two advertisements below and then answer the questions which follow.

THE NO-INSTALLATION TOTAL HOME SECURITY SYSTEM FOR ONLY £59.95

The Spyball Intruder Alarm is a remarkable new home security system that requires no wiring or complicated installation - yet offers complete protection against intruders in an area up to 1000 sqm (average size of 4 bedroom house) all around your home - for just £59.95. It works on the simple principle of air pressure changes within your home. As soon as an outside door or window is opened or forced, a piercing 110 dB alarm is triggered, which sounds for $3^1/_2$ minutes to scare off potential intruders, before re-setting. Spyball is easy to live with - you can move around freely inside your home while it's on, and it won't be set off by open letter-boxes or cat-flaps. Other features include 60-second exit delay, variable entry delay and sensitivity controls, key arming (with 2 keys supplied, additional available) and LED-armed and low-battery indicator light. Compact 6" x 6" free-standing or wall-mounted control unit comes with fittings and window deterrent stickers supplied. Powered by 8 × AA batteries (not supplied).

Spyball Intruder Alarm £59.95 UE616D

SECURITY LIGHT ONLY £29.95

The Security Light uses the latest infra-red technology to detect movement over an area you determine, and switches on a pair of floodlights if there's someone in the vicinity. A programmable timer means that the floodlights stay on for between ten seconds and fifteen minutes (or until switched off), making any burglar clearly visible - and giving you plenty of time to find your keys, park your car, or answer the door. The water-resistant unit has a built-in light-sensitive cell that disables the sensor during the day. And unlike many others, our Security Light comes ready to install, complete with junction box. It's a remarkably effective - and incredibly economical - deterrent system. Two floodlight bulbs provide 300 watts of power.

Security System £29.95 UE679
Bulbs (pair) £9.95 UE678

In the photoemissive cell circuit in Fig. 60.1 a current of the order of microamps flows if the light falling on the photocathode has a frequency greater than the threshold frequency for the cathode coating.

FACT FILE

$hf = hf_o + \frac{1}{2}mv^2$ where hf = the energy of the incident photon, hf_o = the work function of the surface, and $\frac{1}{2}mv^2$ = the maximum kinetic energy of the emitted electron.

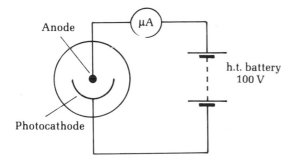

Anode

μA

h.t. battery
100 V

Photocathode

Figure 60.1 A photoemissive cell

1 **a)** What will happen to the current observed as the intensity of the light is increased?
b) Describe, with reasons, what would be observed if the photocell is connected the other way round to the voltage supply and the voltage supply is variable.

2 **a)** If the photocathode material has a work function of 2.8 eV and light of photon energy 3.6 eV is incident on the cathode, calculate the maximum energy of the emitted electrons.
b) What voltage would have to be applied across the cell to stop the electron flow?

3 **a)** Design a circuit incorporating the photo cell to act as a burglar alarm if a light beam is broken by an intruder. Hint: you will need to incorporate a suitable relay circuit.
b) Why might a UV source of light be a good idea for the burglar alarm using a photocell with a cathode–coating work function of 3 eV rather than an infrared source?

4 Other types of burglar alarms include pressure pads or body heat sensors. Design possible circuits for these.

5 Back to photoelectric emission. In an experiment using a photocell, a stopping potential of 1.5 V was observed when monochromatic radiation illuminated a photocell of work function 2.8 eV. The maximum saturation current was 0.005 mA. Find.
a) the energy of each incident photon.
b) the frequency of the incident photons.
c) the number of photoelectrons emitted per second.
d) the threshold frequency for the cathode.

6 What experimental results would you need to take and how would you interpret them in order to verify the photoelectric equation given in the fact file?

ANSWERS

Answers to numerical questions and hints to help with discussion questions.

MECHANICS

1 ▸ AN OPENING PROBLEM OF SOME MOMENT

1 It enables a greater force to be applied without the opener slipping.

2 Diagram needs to show the frictional force at the stopper to keep the opener from slipping, the frictional force between the top and the container and the force applied by the user.
Lever action occurs here so taking moments about the centre of a jar or bottle gives:
force exerted by user × length of arm of opener = force holding jar closed × radius of top. Hence, the force exerted by the user is less than if opening the jar directly.

3 a) It is an indication of the frictional force between the container and its top when it is being unscrewed.
b) Force exerted F_1 × length of opener $d = F \times 0.03$.
Force exerted F_2 × length of opener $d = F \times 0.08$.
Hence, F_1 is smaller than F_2. The bottle will be easier to open than the jar.
c) It is more effective on smaller tops.

4 a) All round grip is achieved on the bottle and it is relatively easy to pull the chain hard.
b) No reduction of force due to lever action.

2 ▸ A QUESTION OF BALANCE

1 The position is balanced if the centre of mass of the system as a whole is directly above P or if the centre of mass of the crane and van alone are above P but it is only stable between these extremes. Grip does not come into the conditions necessary for equilibrium

2 a) Simple proportional treatment will lead to an estimated position of the centre of mass of the van and crane slightly to the right of the vertical line through P.
b) In roughly the position shown in Figure 2.1 (overleaf) for stability.

3 a) (i) Clockwise moment = $2mgx$.
(ii) Anticlockwise moment = mgy.
b) For stability $2mgx < mgy$.

4 a) $T = O$. (The crane will not be lifting the car.)
b) $4T = mg$, giving $T = mg/4$.
c) $mg/4$ and 0.

5 a) $4T + 4r = mg$.
b) $2R = 4T + 2mg$

6 Total reaction at P = $4T + 2mg$
Minimum value occurs when $T = O$, giving total reaction at P = $2mg$.
Maximum value occurs when $4T = mg$, giving total reaction at P = $3mg$.

7 See article.

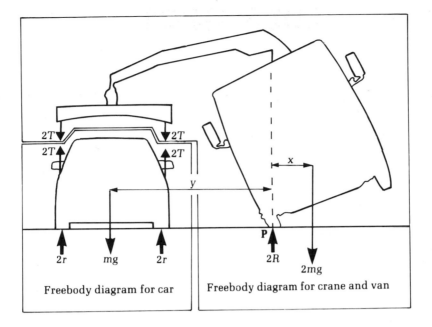

| Freebody diagram for car | Freebody diagram for crane and van |

Figure 2.1

DANGEROUS TIMES

1 $F \times 0.0001 = 0.001 \times 2$, giving $F = 20$ N.

2 a) $10 = 0 + 0.5 \times 10 \times t^2$, giving $t = 1.41$ s.
 b) $v = 0 + 10 \times 1.41 = 14.1$ m s^{-1}.
 c) (Resultant velocity)$^2 = 14.1^2 + 0.5^2$, giving resultant velocity = 14.11 m s^{-1} at an angle of $88°$ to the ground.
 d) Horizontal distance = horizontal velocity $\times$ time = $0.5 \times 1.41 = 0.71$ m.

3 Kinetic energy = $0.5 \times 0.001 \times 14.11^2 = 0.1$ J.

4 If the ground gives for a distance of say 2 mm, the average force exerted as the caterpillar is brought to a stop is given by Force $\times$ distance = energy transformed, giving $F \times 0.002 = 0.1$. Hence, $F = 50$ N.

5 a) Air resistance is significant.
 b) (Resultant velocity)$^2 = 4^2 + 3^2$, giving resultant velocity = 5 m s^{-1} at $36.9°$ to the horizontal.

4 **SAFE DRIVING**

1 a) Reduced frictional forces, increased thinking times.
 b) Reduced awareness of what is going on increases reaction times.

2 a) 8.9 m s^{-1}, 13.3 m s^{-1}, 17.8 m s^{-1}, 22.2 m s^{-1}, 26.7 m s^{-1}, 31.1 m s^{-1}.
 b) 6.6 m s^{-2}, 6.3 m s^{-2}, 6.6 m s^{-2}, 6.5 m s^{-2}, 6.5 m s^{-2}, 6.5 m s^{-2}.

3 Using $Ft = mv - mu$ gives average force = 1.3×10^5 N.

4 Use of crumple zones.

5 a) Total distance moved by driver = $0.15 + 2.74 = 2.89$ m. Average force $\times$ distance = change in energy, giving force of about 1.0×10^4 N.
 b) Allowing driver more movement in seat belt but little overall effect, crashing into a more flexible barrier if there is a choice.

6 Reducing speed limits, bigger crumple zones, better brakes, safety cages, etc.

5 ▶ POLE VAULT AND LONG JUMP

1 *Run up* – pole carried horizontally; *going up* – pole flexed; *top* – body over bar, pole straight; *coming down* – pole falling away; *landing* on large cushioned landing pad – pressed down by body.

2 *Run up*: chemical energy changes to kinetic energy and heat energy in the vaulter's body and in the surrounding air.
Going up: kinetic energy changes to strain energy in pole which changes to kinetic energy (motion now upwards) which changes to gravitational potential energy.
Top of the vault: maximum potential energy, but a little kinetic energy to move over the bar.
Coming down: Gravitational potential energy changes to kinetic energy and heat energy in the surrounding air.
Landing: Kinetic energy changes to strain energy in cushion and sound energy and heat energy.

3 See Figure 5.1.

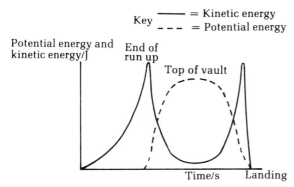

Key ——— = Kinetic energy
- - - = Potential energy

Figure 5.1

4 a) Maximum height gained by the centre of gravity of the vaulter is about 5.1 m, the probable mass is about 80 kg, giving a maximum potential energy gain of approximately 4.1×10^3 J.
b) Greater.
c) The pole vaulter still has some kinetic energy at the top of the vault and some energy is dissipated as heat – in the air, the vaulter's body and the pole. The energy doesn't just disappear due to conservation of energy.

5 a) Greater kinetic energy so more energy available for conversion to potential energy.
b) A pole must be bent by the correct amount to jump the vault successfully. A stiffer pole will store more strain energy for a given bend and so enable the vaulter to go higher.

6 a) Possible average speed of jump = 10 m s⁻¹ so with extra speed of 1.7 m s⁻¹, the total speed relative to the ground = 11.7 m s⁻¹, i.e. an increase of 17%.
b) Actual increase is likely to be much smaller as the body is not a light, horizontal projectile. The body lifts about 1 m during the jump and muscles are used to gain extra distance.

7 Air is less dense so the viscous drag on the body is less. There is also some advantage due to following wind decreasing the effective resistance.

6 ▶ SKY DIVING

1 Weight of skydiver.

2 Total upward force = weight of skydiver = approximately 800 N.

3 a) Upward viscous force, Archimedian upthrust due to displaced air, downward force due to weight.
b) Upward viscous force + Archimedian upthrust due to displaced air = downward force due to weight.

4 The density of air is less at higher altitudes making the Archimedian upthrust due to the displaced air less. Hence, from the equation in 3 b) the upward viscous force must be bigger. As the upward viscous force is proportional to the velocity this may also be bigger provided there is not a significant reduction in the coefficient of viscosity of the air.

5 The problem here is essentially one of conservation of momentum. If one skydiver approaches another directly at speed the effect of the collision may send the previously 'stationary' skydiver away (stationary in a horizontal sense only!).
A good technique is for the extra skydiver to approach the ring tangentially and as slowly as possible.

6 a) Terminal velocity $= 100$ mph $= 44.4$ m s^{-1}.

$$6\pi r \eta v + \frac{4}{3}\pi r^3 \rho g = mg$$

so assuming the skydiver is approximately a sphere of radius 1 m, we have

$$6\pi \times 1 \times \eta \times 44.4 + \frac{4}{3}\pi \times 1 \times 1.1 \times 10 = 800$$

giving $\eta = 0.90$ kg m^{-1} s^{-1}.
b) The diver's shape cannot be approximated to that of a sphere. Also the flow of air may be turbulent and not streamlined.

7 a) As before, plus a large upward force due to the air resistance introduced by the parachute.
b) There is acceleration to the terminal velocity. This continues until the parachute is opened when there is an initial sharp deceleration which gradually decreases until a new lower terminal velocity is reached. This is followed by deceleration on landing to a final zero velocity.

7 HELICOPTER MANOEUVRES

1 a) Lift force = weight $= 1.5 \times 10^4$ N.
b) This must be equal and opposite to the lift force, i.e. action and reaction are equal and opposite.
c) Cross–sectional area of the cylinder of air $= \pi r^2$ $= 28.3$ m^2.
Mass/unit length of cylinder $= 33.9$ kg m^{-1}.
Mass/s moved downwards $= 33.9 \times$ velocity.
Force = rate of change of momentum
= mass/s moved downwards $\times$ velocity
$= 33.9 \times$ (velocity)^2, giving velocity $= 21$ m s^{-1}.

2

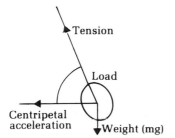

Figure 7.1

When the helicopter banks round, initially, the load continues in a straight line, swinging out from under the helicopter. The load swings out until the horizontal component of the tension in the rope is sufficient to provide the centripetal acceleration and the vertical component of the tension balances the weight of the load.

3 a) 15 km h^{-1} $= 4.2$ m s^{-1}, giving the acceleration $= 1.2$ m s^{-2}.
b) Force $= 1.2 \times 10^2$ N.

4 $T\cos \varnothing = 1.2 \times 10^2$, $T\sin \varnothing = 1000$, giving:
a) $\tan \varnothing = 8.333$, so $\varnothing = 83.2°$
b) $T = 1007$ N.

5 a) Struts about 2 m apart, mass of the keeper about 80 kg, so $\tan \varnothing = 0.2$, giving:
a) $\varnothing = 11.3°$
b) $2T\sin \varnothing = 800$, so tension $= 2040$ N.

6

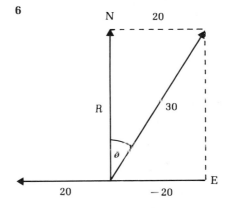

Figure 7.2

a) $\sin \varnothing = 0.6667$, so $\varnothing = $ N 41.8° E.
b) $R^2 = 30^2 - 20^2$, giving resultant speed $= 22$ km h^{-1}.

7 a) Speed on outward journey relative to ground $= 35$ km h^{-1}, giving a time of 17 minutes.
b) Speed on return journey relative to ground $= 25$ km h^{-1}, giving a time of 24 minutes.

8 AUTOMATIC WASHING MACHINES

1 They act as a suspension for the drums, allowing them to vibrate slightly when forced.

2 The increase in mass will reduce the amplitude of any oscillations that might build up during washing or spinning.

3 a) 21.7 Hz, 16.7 Hz, 13.3 Hz, 6.7 Hz, 0.83 Hz.
b) Frequency with which the body vibrates after it has been displaced and then released.
The machine will have a greater tendency to vibrate at this frequency.

4 The natural period of vibration is 1.2 s. We do not want a spring with the same period of oscillation at 5 kg loading. This is the one with a spring constant of 137 N m^{-1}.

5 As wet clothes whirl around in the spin dryer, the wall of the drum exerts a force on the clothes in a direction towards the centre of the drum. This centripetal force causes the clothes to keep moving in a circle. Where there are holes in the drum, the water experiences no push towards the centre of the drum and continues to move tangentially escaping through the holes.

6 Assume the radius of the drum is 200 cm. $\omega = 2\pi f$ and $F = mr\omega^2$, giving the centripetal forces = 1.85×10^3 N, 1.10×10^3 N, 7.02×10^2 N, 1.75×10^2 N.

7 a) The forces holding the remaining water in the clothes are sufficient to provide the centripetal force needed to keep the remaining water moving round in a circle at the low spin speed.
b) Get more evaporation by hanging on a line or tumble drying or using a higher spin speed.
c) Natural fibres are more absorbant due to their structure.

9 ANTIQUE CLOCKS

1 a) (i) 0.57 m.
(ii) 1.01 m.
b) Lack of space?
c) It is not really a simple pendulum as the rod supporting the bob has significant mass. The formula is only approximate for a simple pendulum.

2 a) At either end of the swing.
b) In the centre of the swing.
c) At either end of the swing.

3 a) Standard derivation to give $\frac{1}{2}m\omega^2a^2$.
b) The motion is not in a straight line.
c) 1.6×10^{-2} J.

WAVE MOTION

10 POLARISED WAVES - PROBLEM OR HELP?

1 a) Fringes get closer together.
b) Points of weakness can be identified and improved designs tested.

2 a) Polaroid is made of long aligned molecules which can be orientated in sunglasses to absorb polarised or partially polarised reflections of sunlight and so cut out glare.

b) Some light coming into the car will be plane polarised from reflections and the action of the stressed screen gives rise to the fringes.

3 a) Light is initially unpolarised. When it passes through the first sheet it becomes polarised in one plane. When the polarised light is incident on a second sheet with an axis of polaroid at 90° to first sheet, all the light is absorbed. No light reaches the eye.

b) If crossed initially: darkness at 0° increasing to maximum brightness at 90° then decreasing to darkness at 180°, followed by brightness at 270° and darkness at 360°.

c) This is possibly due to a combination of interference and different degrees of rotation of polarisation according to stress.

4 Stressed plastic film is stretched over glass pieces. According to the direction of stress when the glass is made into a jigsaw, different colours are seen when viewed through the crossed polaroids.

5 See text. Basically, the electric field provides changes in polarisation of different segments, changing the light reflected from a mirror behind the liquid crystal.

6 a) Adjust the polaroids until dark, insert the solution, rotate the analyser until dark again, note the angle turned.

b) Can be used to monitor the strength of solutions in manufacturing processes using optically–active solutions.

11 SEISMIC WAVES

1 Waves are transverse where the direction of vibration is perpendicular to the direction of propagation.
Waves are longitudinal where the direction of vibration is parallel to the direction of propagation.

2 a) The epicentre is the point of origin of the disturbance leading to the earthquake.
The Richter scale is a scale giving an idea of the severity of the event.

b) Outside, there is less danger from falling, unsafe buildings. Further damage is produced in the after shocks.
Changes in land level, buidings not specifically designed to withstand earthquakes of this scale, etc.

c) Regions of intense geological activity, found at plate margins.

3 P wave velocity = 5.6×10^3 ms^{-1}.
S wave velocity = 3.3×10^3 ms^{-1}.
P waves will arrive first.

4 a) $\sin 20/\sin r = 6.1/8.1$, giving $r = 27°$.

b) The P wave should be totally internally reflected. Critical angle $\emptyset = 48.9°$.

5 S waves will not be transmitted if the core is liquid so the shadow of S waves shown is evidence for a liquid core in the Earth.

6 a) $5611t = s$ and $3333(t + 120) = s$
therefore, $s = 9.9 \times 10^2$ km.

b) The waves follow the same path.

7 It must increase faster than the density increases so that the velocity in successively deeper rock layers increases.

12 SPECTRA AND STARS

1 a) Wavelength gets smaller.

b) Wavelength gets larger.

2 a) Wavelength = 3×10^{-11} m.

b) $\Delta\lambda = 4.57 \times 10^{-14}$ m.

3 These are due to absorption of light at certain frequencies by the gases in the star's atmosphere. This light is then emitted in all directions leading to a reduction in the light travelling towards the observer from the star. The frequencies are determined by the elements in the star's atmosphere. Each element has a characteristic pattern. If the pattern observed is at frequencies greater or less than expected the star is moving towards or away from the observer.

4 The observer sees the bright emission spectra due to the elements in the Sun's atmosphere which h give lines at exactly the same frequencies.

5 a) $f = 1/T = 3.47 \times 10^{-5}$ Hz.

b) $w = 2\pi f = 2.18 \times 10^{-4}$ rad s^{-1}.

c) $v = wr$, therefore $r = 2 \times 10^9$ m.

d) $a = rw^2 = 99.7$ ms^{-2}.

6 Small and dark.

13 MUSICAL INSTRUMENTS

1 a) Stringed instruments, timpani.

b) Wind instruments, e.g. brass and woodwind.

c) They are the same..

d) (i) Air in body of violin.
(ii) Air in body of drum.
(iii) Sounding board.
(iv) Trumpet end and tube.

2 a)

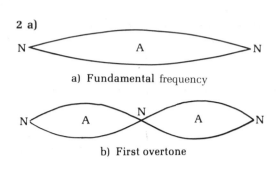

a) Fundamental frequency

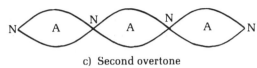

b) First overtone

c) Second overtone

Figure 13.1 Vibrating string

b) $f = v/2l$; v/l; $3v/2l$.

3 a)

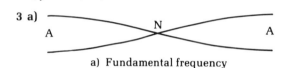

a) Fundamental frequency

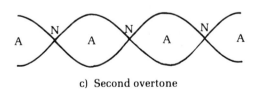

b) First overtone

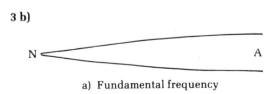

c) Second overtone

Figure 13.2 Open pipe

3 b)

a) Fundamental frequency

Figure 13.3 Closed pipe

b) First overtone

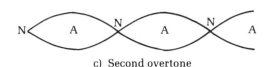

c) Second overtone

Figure 13.3 continued

c) For an open pipe: $f = v/2l$; v/l; $3v/2l$, respectively. For a closed pipe: $f = v/4l$; $3v/4l$; $5v/4l$, respectively.

4 a) As there must be a node at the closed end the even harmonics are missing.
As there must be antinodes at the open ends the odd harmonics are missing.
b) Quality depends on the different percentages of the overtones present. With different overtones available in the different pipes, different sounds will be produced.

5 a) $l/4 = 2$, therefore $l = 8$ m, giving a frequency of 42.5 Hz.
b) $l/2 = 2$, therefore $l = 4$ m, giving a frequency of 85 Hz.
c) If both pipes are closed at one end, the frequency of the second pipe = 40.5 Hz, giving a beat frequency of $42.5 - 40.5 = 2$ Hz.
If both pipes are open, the frequency of the second pipe = 81 Hz, giving a beat frequency of 4 Hz.
d) Probably, as a variation in loudness should be detectable at these frequencies.

6 a) Violin = 0.52 m, viola = 0.77 m, cello = 1.6 m.
b) Tension = 63 N.

7 a) There is one loop between two nodes, so the phase will be the same for all parts of the string and the amplitude will vary from zero at a node to a maximum at the antinode in the centre of the loop.
b) There are two loops so there will be a node in the centre of the string and a node at each end. Parts of the string in the first loop are 180° out of phase with parts in the second loop. The amplitude will again be varying from zero at the nodes to a maximum at the antinodes. Now, there will be zero amplitude in the centre of the vibrating string.

14 REFLECTIVE TOYS AND INSTRUMENTS

1 a)

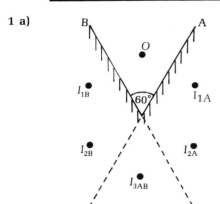

Figure 14.1 Images in a kaleidoscope. Mirrors at 60° give five images

b) The number of images will decrease.

c) The number of images will increase.

d) Theoretically, an infinite number. But, there is some absorption of light at each reflection which means that the number visible is limited.

2 a) Erect.

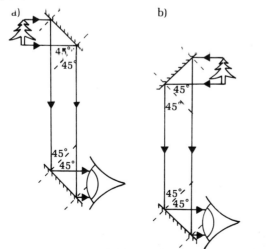

Figure 14.2 a) Forward and b) rear viewing mirror periscopes

b) Rearrange the mirrors as in the diagram.

c) Upside–down.

3 a) The reflected ray is rotated through twice the angle, i.e. 60°.

b) In reverse, initially AO is reflected along OH. When the mirror is rotated through ø, AO is reflected along OS. You showed in 3a) that the reflected ray moves through twice the angle of rotation of the mirror. Therefore, ø is half the angle of elevation of the Sun.

4 a) For sanity whilst driving, the image must be erect.

b) Multiple reflections are possible between the front and back of a mirror giving multiple imaging. With total internal reflection in a prism there is only one reflection.

c)

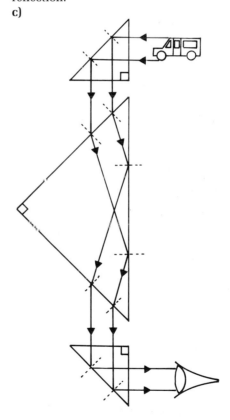

Figure 14.3 Rear viewing prism periscope

d) From refraction at the first face with $i = 45°$ (see diagram) $r = 28.1°$. From the geometry of the figure, i at the second face is $73.1°$, giving total internal reflection at the second face, as i is bigger than the critical angle for the glass. Hence, by symmetry, there is an emergent angle of $45°$.

5 It gives a wider field of view.

a)

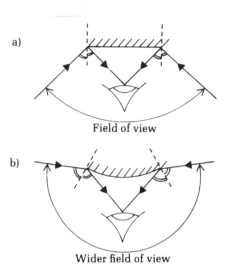

Field of view

b)

Wider field of view

Figure 14.4

6 Refraction, dispersion and total internal reflections.

7 Mirror length needed = 0.85 m and it will need to be placed as shown in the diagram.

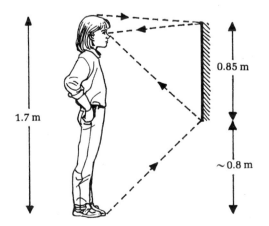

0.85 m

1.7 m

~0.8 m

Figure 14.5 Placing the mirror

15 ULTRASOUND IMAGING

1 a) Wavelength in bone = 2.04 mm.
b) Wavelength in soft tissue = 0.75 mm.

2 a) Air $Z = 429$ kg m^{-2} s^{-1}, soft tissue $Z = 1.59 \times 10^6$ kg m^{-2} s^{-1}, bone $Z = 6.94 \times 10^6$ kg m^{-2} s^{-1}.
b) For a soft tissue/bone interface, $a = 0.39$.
For an air/soft tissue interface, $a = 0.999$.
Almost all the ultrasound will be reflected at an air/soft tissue boundary, whereas only 0.39 of the incident ultrasound will be reflected in the case of a soft tissue/bone interface.

3 $\sin i / \sin r = v_1 / v_2$, where v_1 is the velocity in the first medium and v_2 is the velocity in the second medium.
Sin 30/sin r = 1450/1590, therefore $r = 33.25°$.
The beam of ultrasound will be bent away from the normal during refraction from fat to muscle. Some of the beam will be reflected in the fat layer at an angle of reflection of 30°.

4 The lens should be concave as ultrasound passing from a liquid to a solid generally increases in velocity and so is bent away from the normal.

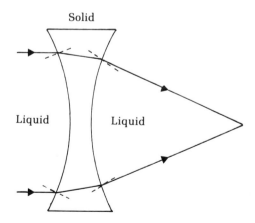

Figure 15.1 Converging lens for ultrasound

5 See article. Limitations arise from the scanning probe causing pressure problems in some parts of the body, e.g. it cannot be used on the eyes. Also, definition problems occur from multiple reflections producing false images. The size of the beam also limits resolution.

6 Very accurate focusing is needed so that the power is not being applied in the wrong place.

7 Total distance travelled = 38.25 m, therefore shoal depth = 19.1 m.

16 ▶ RAINBOWS

1 a) There is always some reflection at an interface between two media of different refractive indices.
b) sin c = 1/1.33, therefore c = 48.8°.

2 139° 43' − 137° 58' = 1° 45'.

3 The crucial factor here is the rainbow angle giving the same angle from different parts of the rainbow to the eye. If the land didn't get in the way we would see a complete circle!

4 a) Ray **a** is reflected from the surface of the drop; ray **b** is refracted twice as it passes through the drop; ray **c** is refracted, internally reflected once, and then refracted out of the drop.
b) Rays **b** and **c**.

5

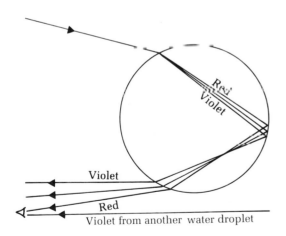

Figure 16.1 Establishing the colours of the rainbow

6 a) Soap bubbles, oil films, jewellery, etc.
b) No. They can be due to interference.

7 a) sin 30/sin r = 1.510 for red light, therefore r = 19.34° sin 30/sin r = 1.521 for blue light, therefore r = 19.19°. Dispersion = 19.34 − 19.19 = 0.15°

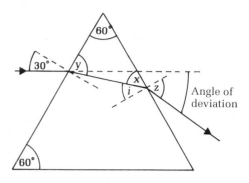

Figure 16.2

b) For the red light, y = 90 − 19.34 = 70.66°, therefore x = 180 − (60 + 70.66) = 49.34°.
New angle of incidence at second face of prism = 90 − 49.34 = 40.66°, therefore final angle of refraction z = 79.69°.
Angle of deviation = total angle turned by ray = (30 − 19.34) + (79.69 − 40.66) = 49.69°.
c) For the blue light, y = 90 − 19.19 = 70.81°, therefore x = 180 − (60 + 70.81) = 49.19°.
New angle of incidence at second face of prism = 90 − 49.19 = 40.81°, therefore final angle of refraction z = 83.75°.
Angle of deviation = total angle turned by ray = (30 − 19.19) + (83.75 - 40.81) = 53.75°.
d) Angular dispersion = 53.75 − 49.69 = 4.06°.

17 ▶ FIBRE OPTICS IN MEDICINE

1 The endoscope enables doctors to look for problems within the body without doing an exploratory operation.

2 a) Light is refracted out through the side of the fibre into the cladding.
b) If the tube is bent through too great an angle, $\phi < \phi_c$.

3

$$n_o \sin i = n_f \sin r = n_f \sin(\frac{\pi}{2} - \phi) = n_f \cos \phi = n_f \sqrt{1 - \sin^2 \phi}$$

4 $n_o \sin i = n_f \sqrt{1 - \sin^2 \phi}$ and $\phi = \phi_c$, therefore

$\sin^2 \phi = \sin^2 \phi_c = \dfrac{n_c^2}{n_f^2}$ and $i = i_{max}$, therefore

$n_o \sin i_{max} = n_f \sqrt{1 - \dfrac{n_c^2}{n_f^2}}$, so $n_o \sin i_{max} = \sqrt{n_f^2 - n_c^2}$.

5 a) Numerical aperture = $(1.58^2 - 1.45^2)^{0.5} = 0.63$.

Half angle = $\dfrac{\sin^{-1} 0.63^2}{1} = 38.9°$.

b) Numerical aperture stays the same.

Half angle = $\sin^{-1}(\dfrac{0.63}{1.33})^2 = 28.2°$, i.e. the half angle changes.

6 a) Coherent bundle - fibres are in the same relative position throughout the bundle so images can be transmitted along it. Incoherent bundle - fibres can be in any order anywhere.

b) More detail is obtained with a smaller diameter fibre.

7 Absorption in the glass itself, absorption at each reflection, scattering by the glass fibre, losses at entry and exit to the fibre.

18 THE HUBBLE TELESCOPE

1 Spherical aberration.

2 NASA set wrong specifications. Contractors made the mirrors to the wrong specifications (i.e. not those set by NASA).

3 a) $u = 10.5$ cm, $f = 10$ cm, hence $v = 210$ cm.
b) $u = 10.51$ cm, $f = 10$ cm, hence $v = 206.1$ cm.
c) 0.1% increase.
d) 1.9% change.
e) Change in magnification = 0.39. % change = 2%.

4 The error is large compared to the current accuracy achievable. Also, see the effect of small movement in Question 3.

5 There are problems in the manufacture of large lenses. It is difficult to get all the glass of optical quality. Also, glass can flow under its own weight.

6 A telescope in space can use the ultraviolet spectrum and achieve better spatial resolution than on Earth.

7 On reflection at the mirror every part of the wave would be reflected back in exactly the reverse direction at the same time.

19 SPECTACLES

1 Ray diagrams showing:
a) the action of a diverging lens plus the eye cornea/lens system bringing the final image of a distant object to a focus on the retina.
b) the action of a converging lens plus the eye cornea/lens system bringing the image of a near object to a focus on the retina.

2 a) Ideas in support of contact lenses may include the greater field of view, use in sport, ease of wearing compared with spectacles.
b) Ideas against contact lenses may include problems of tolerance, cleaning and sterilisation, putting them in and taking them out, and the difficulties of complex prescriptions.

3 The sharp line between the two parts of the lens can cause a 'blind spot' and give a false impression of what is viewed.

4 a) Probably D–shaped bifocals or executive bifocals would be best, as the need for quick interchange between near and distant objects is paramount.
b) Varifocals have a much narrower field of vision than would be required.

5 When an object is at the least distance of distinct vision a correcting lens will need to produce a virtual image at 40 cm. This will then be seen in focus by the eye system. So, $u = 25$ cm and $v = -40$ cm, hence $f = 66.7$ cm and the power of the lens = 1.5 dioptres.

6 a) A correcting lens will need to produce a virtual image at 20 cm of a distant object at infinity. This will then be seen in focus by the eye system. So, $u = \infty$ and $v = -20$ cm hence $f = -20$ cm and the power of the lens = −5 dioptres.
b) If $f = -20$ cm and $v = -10$ cm, then $u = 20$ cm. So using this lens a book could be placed 20 cm from the eye and an image will be formed at the eye's near point. This is reasonable for comfortable reading. Bifocals will probably not be necessary.

7 a) From the thickness: thicker in the middle compared to the edges = converging, thinner in the middle compared to the edges = diverging.
b) Gives increased field of view.

20 USING A CAMERA

1 The aperture area doubles and the exposure time halves.

2 The depth of field is the range of object distances which appear in focus in a particular shot. The smaller the aperture the greater the depth of field.

3 a) 50 mm.
b) $50/d = 5.6$, giving $d = 8.9$ mm.

4 $u = 0.25$ m, $f = 0.05$ m, giving $v = 0.0625$ $m = 62.5$ mm. Hence, the optical centre of the lens must be moved 12.5 mm away from the film.

5 a) By changing the separation of the different components.
b) 50 mm.
c) $u = 3$ m, $f = 0.03$ m or 0.08 m, giving $v = 30.3$ mm or 82.2 mm, so range of movement = 51.9 mm.

6 a) Each increase of the f–number doubles the exposure time, so the time = $16/250 = 6.4 \times 10^{-2}$ s.
b) Increased depth of focus but less opportunity to get a sharp image of a moving object with the longer exposure and greater chance of camera shake.

7 Infrared photography for heat losses and archeology, medical photography via optic fibres, x-ray photography etc.

21 CONCERT HALLS

1 Your diagram needs to show how sound might get to the listener's ear both directly and after several reflections round the hall, so giving suffient time between the signals for them to be distinguished. Sound absorbing materials on the walls would reduce this problem as would baffles introduced to intercept the reflections.

2 The listener could experience destructive interference or constructive interference at certain frequencies between reflected sound waves and directly received ones.

3 Applying the formula in the article gives reverberation times of 1.47 s, 1.84 s and 2.21 s.

4 Examples could include the use of glass fibre wedges in sound proofing, double glazing, soft furnishings, cavity–wall fillings and rubber mats for typewriters.

5 The screen is acting as a diffraction grating. Using $d \sin \phi = n\lambda$ gives the angle ϕ to the straight through direction where the sound can be heard the loudest (constructive interference). This gives $\phi = 26.1°$ and $61.6°$.

22 CRYSTALLOGRAPHY

1 a) The umbrella fabric is acting as an approximate two–dimensional diffraction grating with the gaps in the weave acting as the 'slits'.
b) Using $d \sin \phi = \lambda$ for first order diffraction gives an angle of 0.13° if a spacing of 0.25 mm is assumed.

2 a) The ring patterns are a diffraction phenomenon and this will only occur if the material structure has points of concentration of matter.
b) The separation of the rings can give information about the crystal structure using the Bragg equation.
c) Diffraction and interference are wave phenomena.

3 See any standard text.

4 Using $2d\sin \phi = n\lambda$, the separation d as 0.26 nm.

5 a) The potential energy = $eV = 1.6 \times 10^{-19} \times 15 \times 10^3$ $= 2.4 \times 10^{-15}$ J. This is the kinetic energy of the electron before striking the target.
b) Using kinetic energy = $1/2\, mv^2$ gives the speed = 7.3×10^7 ms^{-1}.
c) Momentum = $mv = 6.6 \times 10^{-23}$ N s.

6 a) $\lambda = h/p$ gives the wavelength is 9.99×10^{-3} nm.
b) 2.86×10^{-4}°.
c) Suppose a first order diffraction angle of 2° is needed, then this gives a grating spacing $d = 0.29$ nm.

7 a) Suppose the person has a speed of 10 m s^{-1} and a mass of 80 kg. The momentum = $mv = 800$ Ns giving the associated wavelength, using $h/p = \lambda$ as 8.25×10^{-37} m.
Using the equation $d \sin \phi = \lambda$ and assuming a door width of 0.75 m, gives $\phi = 6.3 \times 10^{-35}$ degrees.
b) This is too small a spread to observe!
c) The shorter associated wavelength of the electron beam will enable appreciable diffraction effects to be observed at smaller values of d in the diffraction equation.

23 ▸ LOUDSPEAKER DESIGN

1 Good stands reduce the vibration of the whole unit. These vibrations can distort the waves emitted.

2 a) The waves on the line AB are exactly half a wavelength out of step with the corresponding waves on the other half BC of the line ABC.
b) See any standard text for single slit diffraction.

3 a) Using $d\sin\phi = \lambda$ gives 2ϕ = angular spread = $61.7 \times 2 = 123.3°$,
b) $2\phi = 15.2°$.

4 By using speakers with smaller diameters for the higher frequencies.

5 For classical music, an even response over all frequencies is desirable while other types of music may sound better with certain frequency ranges slightly emphasised.

ELECTRICITY, FIELDS AND ELECTROMAGNETISM

24 ▸ A HAND DRYER

1 a) A motor driven fan and a heater.
b) It must be in parallel in this case as 240 V is dropped across each.

2 9A.

3 a) Power = $VI = 2.16 \times 10^3$ W.
b) 240 W.

4 Total power = 2400 W. Suppose the heater is on for one minute for each passenger. Total time that the heater is switched on during the week is $120 \times 6 \times 1 = 720$ minutes = 12 hrs. Total energy used = 28.8 kWh. If one unit costs 8 p, the total cost = £2.30.

5 Peak value = $240\sqrt{2} = 339$ V.

6 The resistance of the heater will increase with temperature.

7 As the coil of the motor rotates, a back e.m.f. is induced which increases to a steady value. The motor current I is given by $V - E = IR$ where V = the applied p.d., E = the induced e.m.f. and R = the motor resistance. As the speed of the motor increases, E increases so $V - E$ decreases and hence I decreases until the motor reaches a maximum constant speed.

25 ▸ CAR LIGHTING CIRCUIT

1 a) 1.75 A or 0.42 A, 0.42 A, 0.42 A, 5.0 A or 4.6 A, 1.75 A.
b) The resistance of each filament will be less when the lamp is cold.

2 They are in parallel so that if one fails the others still operate.

3 a) 2.08 A.
b) 16.5 A

4 The generator, which is a dynamo, is recharging the battery.

5 a) 6.86 Ω or 28.8 Ω, 28.8 Ω, 28.8 Ω, 2.4 Ω or 2.62 Ω, 6.86 Ω.
b) $R = V/I = 12/16.5 = 0.73$ Ω.

6 a) Total wattage is 25 W, so energy dissipated = $25 \times 10 \times 3600 = 9.0 \times 10^5$ J.
b) Energy dissipated to run the battery flat = $12 \times 1 \times 24 \times 3600 = 1.0 \times 10^6$ J. Yes, the car will still start. Typical starter motor draws about 100A from a 12V battery.

7 a) (i) By considering resistors in parallel the single equivalent resistor R to the lights = 5.76 Ω.

$E = Ir + IR$ gives the total current $I = 1.55$ A, so the current through each bulb = 0.31 A.
(ii) $V = IR$ gives 8.93 V across each lamp.
(iii) New working power = $8.93 \times 0.31 = 2.77$ W.
b) It would be considerably reduced.

26 POWER TRANSMISSION

1 a) Power supplied = power wasted + power available at the load.
b) $V_{in}I = I^2R + V_{out}I$.

2 Strategies can include using cables of a low resistance and transmitting at high voltages to reduce the current in the cables.

3 a) With a high cross–sectional area the weight of the cables will increase.
b) By using materials of low resistivity and low density.

4 a) $V_{in}I = I^2R + V_{out}I$, $V_{in} = IR + V_{out}$, so $6 = 3I + 6I$, therefore giving $I = 0.67$ A.
b) Power loss = $I^2R = 1.33$ W.
c) $V_{in}I = I^2R + V_{out}I$, therefore power available = $4 - 1.33 = 2.67$ W.

5 a) Weight: copper = 1.8×10^{-2} kg or 7.0×10^{-1} kg; Aluminium = 5.3×10^{-3} kg or 2.1×10^{-4} kg; Iron = 1.5×10^{-2} kg or 6.2×10^{-4} kg.
Resistance: copper = $0.87\ \Omega$ or $21.6\ \Omega$; aluminium = $1.38\ \Omega$ or $34.4\ \Omega$; iron = $5.53\ \Omega$ or $134\ \Omega$.
The choice must be between copper and aluminium because of their significantly lower resistance. If weight is also a problem then aluminium is the best compromise.
b) See standard text.

6 a) Using transformers with a turns ratio of 8:1 before and after the supply wires will give a transmission voltage of 48 V. If the transformers are 100% efficient power in = power out giving a new current in the supply wires of 0.083 A.
b) The new power available = $4 - (0.083)^2 \times 3 = 3.98$ W

27 MOSTLY NATURAL SATELLITES

1 a) Similarities: radius of orbit, radius, density, mass. Differences: period of orbit, orbital speed.
b) Orbital speed = $rw = r(2\pi f) = r(2\pi)/T$. This gives 1.02×10^3 m s^{-1} for the Moon and 1.73×10^4 m s^{-1} for the satellite Io.

2 a) The Moon must rotate once about its own axis in the same time as it completes an orbit around the Earth. (If you don't believe this, experiment with an orange for the Earth and a satsuma for the Moon.) Scientists suspect that this occurs because the centre of mass for the moon is not exactly at the geometrical centre of the moon.
b) The period of rotation will be 27.32 days.

3 a) The graph should be a straight line going through the origin.
b) The graph shows that (the period of orbit)^2 is proportional to (the radius of orbit)^3.
c) This is Kepler's third law. Find out about the first two laws!

4 a) $g = -\dfrac{GM}{R^2}$ giving g for Titan as 1.54 m s^{-2}.

This is much less than the Earth's gravity resulting in reduced body weight and bouncing movements.
b) Escape velocity = $\sqrt{2gR} = 2.74$ k m s^{-1}.

5 Scientists may have problems getting their ideas accepted if these ideas do not reflect the main body of current thinking. Today, however, modern communications and ease of travel help to allow the easy interchange of ideas.

6 a) The satellite is orbiting so that its position remains above the same point on the Earth all the time.

b) Acceleration of satellite $a = -\dfrac{GM}{R^2}$ and $g = -\dfrac{GM}{r^2}$

giving $\dfrac{a}{g} = \dfrac{r^2}{R^2}$.

But $a = R\omega^2$, therefore $\dfrac{R\omega^2}{g} = \dfrac{r^2}{R^2}$

$\omega = \dfrac{2\pi}{T}$, therefore $\dfrac{R(2\pi)^2}{gT^2} = \dfrac{r^2}{R^2}$

giving the radius of orbit of the satellite $R = 4.25 \times 10^7$ m.
Therefore, the height above the Earth's surface = 3.62×10^7 m.

7 If the spacecraft is a distance d from the centre of the Earth and the Earth/Moon separation is R, then by considering the forces on the spacecraft:

$\dfrac{GEm}{d^2} = \dfrac{GMm}{(R-d)^2}$ giving $E(R-d)^2 = Md^2$,

where E = the mass of the Earth and M = the mass of the Moon.

28 ▶ THUNDERCLOUDS AND LIGHTNING CONDUCTORS

1 The connection is vital to permit charge flow. Checking during a thunderstorm risks a lightning strike on you.

2 The high electric field at the points causes ionisation of the air molecules close by which are then repelled from the points towards the oppositely charged cloud base.

3 a) There is a large distance from the top to the bottom of the cloud leading to the possibility of the holding of charge separately between the top and the bottom. The thermals may help in the separation of the charge by transporting charge within the cloud.
b) Water droplets or even ice crystals carried in the thermals may be the charge carriers.

4 a) The leader will follow the path of least resistance in the air which need not be straight.
b) Ions in the air and electrons.
c) This is due to the rapid expansion of the air heated by the lightning flash.

5 a) $W_{max} = \dfrac{1}{2}QV = 2.5 \times 10^{10}$ J.
b) That the base of the cloud and the Earth are acting as a parallel plate capacitor.

c) Sound energy, light energy and heat energy.

6 Kite flying in thunderstorms is not a good idea.

7 Take off metal framed rucksacks, come down off high points quickly or lie down, do not shelter under trees.

29 ▶ PLANETS IN THE SOLAR SYSTEM

1 The planets were called wandering stars because their position with respect to other 'stars' changed as viewed from the Earth. The orbit of the planet does not change. The reversal of direction is due to the relative movement of the Earth and the planet.

2 a) The moon is directly between the Earth and the Sun and so the moon blocks out the sunlight.
b) The Earth is directly between the Sun and the moon and casts its shadow on the moon making it look dark.

3 One group is that of the terrestrial planets. These are Mercury, Venus, Earth and Mars. They are all relatively close to the Sun and have a small radius and a high density.

The other group is the outer planets, Jupiter, Saturn, Uranus, Neptune and Pluto. These are characterised by their greater distance from the Sun and, with the exception of Pluto, by a large radius and relatively low density.

4 a) 1.32×10^{-7}, 5.15×10^{-8}, 3.17×10^{-8}, 1.68×10^{-8}, 2.67×10^{-9}, 1.08×10^{-9}, 3.77×10^{-10}, 1.92×10^{-10}, 1.28×10^{-10} Hz.
b) 8.29×10^{-7}, 3.24×10^{-7}, 1.99×10^{-7}, 1.06×10^{-7}, 1.68×10^{-8}, 6.79×10^{-9}, 2.3×10^{-9}, 1.21×10^{-9}, 8.04×10^{-10} rad s^{-1}.
c) $48\,007$, $35\,060$, $29\,770$, $24\,162$, $11\,227$, $9\,689$, $6\,599$, $5\,443$, $4\,743$ ms^{-1}.
d) 0.0398, 0.0114, 5.92×10^{-3}, 2.56×10^{-3}, 1.89×10^{-4}, 6.58×10^{-5}, 1.52×10^{-5}, 6.59×10^{-6}, 3.81×10^{-6} ms^{-2}.
e) Mass of each planet = volume × density = 3.21×10^{23}, 4.85×10^{24}, 6.00×10^{24}, 6.42×10^{23}, 2.02×10^{27}, 6.28×10^{26}, 9.04×10^{25}, 1.03×10^{26} kg.

Force = mass x acceleration =
1.28×10^{22}, 5.53×10^{22}, 3.55×10^{22}, 1.64×10^{21}, 3.82×10^{23}, 4.13×10^{22}, 1.37×10^{21}, 6.79×10^{20}N.

5 Force = $\dfrac{GM_1M_2}{R^2}$ gives for the Earth $3.55 \times 10^{22} =$

$$\dfrac{G \times 335000 \times 6 \times 10^{24} \times 6 \times 10^{24}}{(149.6 \times 10^9)^2},$$

giving $G = 6.59 \times 10^{-11}$ N m² kg⁻².
Accurate value = 6.67×10^{-11} N m² kg⁻².

6 a) (i) Intensity of radiation received on Earth/ intensity of radiation received on Mars = 2.32.
(ii) Intensity of radiation received on Earth/ intensity of radiation received on Jupiter = 20.1.
b) The outer planets would be unlikely to support any life as we know it.

7 Hint: find out about the atmosphere of different planets.

8 a) $g - \dfrac{GM}{R^2}$ giving the Sun's surface gravitation

$$\dfrac{6.7 \times 10^{11} \times 335000 \times 6 \times 10^{24}}{(6.96 \times 10^8)^2} = 278\,ms^{-2}.$$

This is approximately 27.8 times greater than g on Earth.
b) As the Earth is spinning about its axis the net value of g is reduced by an amount equal to the centripetal acceleration.
g at the equator = $9.81 - r\omega^2$

$$= 9.81 - r(2\pi f)^2 = 9.81 - \dfrac{6378 \times 10^3 (2\pi)^2}{(24 \times 60 \times 60)^2} = 9.78\,ms^{-2}.$$

9 a) See standard text.

b) Escape velocity = $\dfrac{\sqrt{2GM}}{\sqrt{r}}$ giving an escape velocity for the Earth of 11 km s⁻¹ and an escape velocity for Mars of $5.05 \times 10^3\,ms^{-1}$.

30   UNDERGROUND CURRENTS

1 The alkaline fluid will contain positive and negative ions, such as OH⁻, which will act as charge carriers.

2 Suitable conditions for ion formation could have occurred as land masses collided as the Earth's plates moved. The currents would then have been induced by the Earth's changing magnetic field. (*See* Faraday's Laws of Electromagnetic Induction in any standard text.)

3 If the current depth varies from 15 to 45 km, take the average depth of the actual current as 30 km and the average width as 125 km, giving a cross-sectional area of 3750 km². This gives a current density of

$$\dfrac{1 \times 10^{-13}}{3750 \times 10^6} = 2.7 \times 10^{-13}\,\mathrm{Am}^{-2}.$$

4 The current density J = nev gives the number density

$$n = \dfrac{2.7 \times 10^{-13}}{1.6 \times 10^{-19} \times 10^{-4}} = 1.69 \times 10^{10}\,m^{-3}.$$

5 They may provide a means of finding deposits of oil and gas.

31   INK JET PRINTING

1 There are very few moving parts

2 a) Only a minute change of charge will result in quite a large change of deflection.
b) Your diagram needs to show the vertical downward force due to the drop's weight, the horizontal force due to the electric field, and an upward force due to air resistance and buoyancy.

3 a) and **b)**

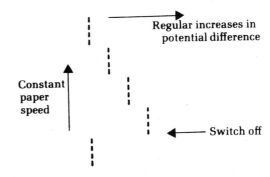

Regular increases in potential difference

Constant paper speed

Switch off

Figure 31.1

4 a) Force $= QE = 4 \times 10^{-8} \times \dfrac{2 \times 10^3}{0.1} = 0.8$ mN.

b) $mg = 0.1 \times 10^{-3} \times 10 = 10^{-3}$ N.

c) $s = \dfrac{1}{2}gt^2$, giving $t = \dfrac{\sqrt{2s}}{\sqrt{g}} = \dfrac{\sqrt{(2 \times 5 \times 10^{-2})}}{\sqrt{10}} = 0.1$s

5 a) $F = ma$, giving sideways acceleration

$= \dfrac{8 \times 10^{-4}}{10^{-4}} = 8\,\mathrm{m\,s^{-2}}$.

Distance deflected sideways in

$0.1\mathrm{s} = \dfrac{1}{2}at^2 = \dfrac{1}{2} \times 8 \times 10^{-2} = 4 \times 10^{-2}$ m $= 4$cm.

b) Velocity sideways as drop leaves plates $= at$ $= 0.8\,\mathrm{ms^{-1}}$. Velocity downwards as it leaves plate $= gt$ $= 1$ m s^{-1}.

Downwards $s = ut + \dfrac{1}{2}at^2$, giving $0.1 = t + \dfrac{1}{2} \times 10t^2$,

therefore $t = 7.3 \times 10^{-2}$ s.
Further deflection sideways $= 0.8 \times 0.73 = 0.0584$ m
$= 5.84$ cm.
Total deflection $= 9.84$ cm.

6 a) Perspex screen in front of the apparatus, warning notice 'high voltage', no touching of the leads or the syringe after switching on.
b) Cut outs and earthed and insulated shields.

32 IONISERS AND DUST PRECIPITATORS

1 a) Negative; as electons are repelled.
b) Positive; as the negatively–charged dust particles are attracted.

2 The field lines should start on the plates from evenly spaced points and end on the wires, giving a concentration of field lines at each wire.

3 They will have acquired some positive charge possibly through colliding with positive ions of air.

4 a) Presumably, some sort of field is being set up to give positive and negative ions which may then be mechanically swept into the room via a fan. If no fan is being used positively and negatively–charged points could give rise to streams of differently charged particles.

b) Again a fan circulating the air could achieve this or the filter could be charged to produce a similar effect to the precipitator.

5 Sulphur dioxide is a gas and, even if ionised, would remain a gas and escape.

6 It is difficult to see how a small ioniser could completely do all four things in a room but it might have some effect.

33 INSIDE THE ATOM

1 The problem about the electron microscope is that we see diffraction patterns due to the interaction of the electron beam and the atoms. We do not see the atoms themselves.

2 a) See standard text. It gave evidence for the Rutherford model.
b) Taking the volume of an atom as that of a sphere of radius 10^{-10} m gives a volume of $4 \times 10^{-30}\,\mathrm{m^3}$. Take the mass as approximately $4 \times 1.67 \times 10^{-27}$ kg. The density of a helium atom is approximately 1670 kg m^{-3}.
Using a radius of 10^{-15} m for a nucleus gives a density of 1.670×10^{18} kg m^{-3}.
The atom must consist largely of empty space.
c) See standard text.

3 a) They will spiral inwards
b) Possibly gaining in speed.

4 a) Using the formula in the fact file gives 0.023 µN
b) 1.01×10^{-47} N.
c) The electrostatic attraction.

5 a) α-particle emission.
b) Assuming a separation of 10^{-15} m gives a repulsive force $= 230$ N.
c) Assuming a separation of 10^{-15} m gives an attractive force $= 1.86 \times 10^{-34}$ N
d) They ought to separate fast!

6 It is called the strong force. It is assumed to have a short range as it is not detected outside the nucleus. It is an exchange force which operates through the interchange of exchange particles called gluons.

7 They are both nuclear models with a central nucleus to the atom. But, in the Bohr model the electron can only orbit the atom in particular orbits determined by quantum conditions imposed on the orbital angular momentum of the electron. The electron does not radiate energy when in these orbits.

34 ELECTRICAL MACHINES

1 The capacitance of the whole system was increased enabling more charge to be stored, so giving a bigger spark.

2 The hand held jar provided the earthed 'plate' of the capacitor, the inner foil or wire provided the plate for charging and the glass provided the dielectric in between.

3 a) (i), (ii) and (iii) In all cases the capacitance increases and the potential reduces.
b) By using a gold leaf electroscope.

4 By using bigger jars and thinner glass.

5 You connect them in parallel as this will give a larger combined capacitance.

6 a) $Q = CV$ therefore $Q = 5 \times 10^{-5}$ C.

Energy $= \frac{1}{2}QV$, therefore energy $= 2.5 \times 10^{-4}$ J.

b) Capacitors in parallel so new combined capacitance $= 7\ \mu F$.
$V = Q/C$, therefore $V = 7.14$ V.

c) Final energy $= \frac{1}{2}QV = 1.8 \times 10^{-4}$ J.

A current has flowed leading to energy changes to heat.

7 a) To get maximum charge and 6V across each you need the capacitors arranged so that one pair in series are in parallel with the other two in series and the battery is in parallel with both pairs.
b) The capacitance of one pair in series is given by

$$\frac{1}{C} = \frac{1}{C_1} + \frac{1}{C_2},$$ giving $C = 50\ \mu F$ for one pair.

The total capacitance = 100 μF.
So, the charge stored $= CV = 100 \times 12 = 1200$ μC.

35 METERING

1 Without measurement and control of electricity we cannot use it. Without using it there would be: no electric light or heat or motive power, no late working in factories, reduced use of world resources, reduced pollution, no heart pacemakers/scanners, no radio or TV, no telephones, no satellites, no atomic power or weapons, no computers, no electric guitars, no rock bands, no cars or aircraft, etc.

2 a) 0.526 Ω
b) 0.101 Ω
c) 0.0503 Ω
d) 0.01 Ω

3 a) 10 Ω
b) 90 Ω
c) 190 Ω
d) 990 Ω

4

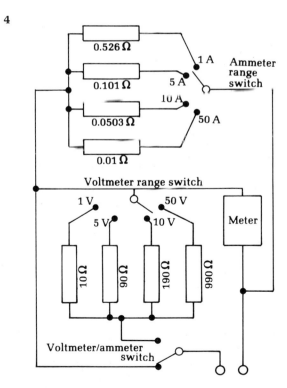

Figure 35.1

5 a) By using a full wave rectifier.

b) See standard text for diagram.

c) For frequency values greater than 10 Hz it will be the r.m.s. value.

36 COSMIC RAYS AND HALL PROBES

1 a) It will move in a circle.

b) It will move in a spiral of half the radius of the circle in a) above (see standard text).

2 a) The cosmic rays spiral along the Earth's magnetic field lines and get funnelled towards the poles.

b) This is complex, but essentially, charged particles can be trapped in closed orbits due to the forces experienced as they move in the Earth's magnetic field, so leading to a build–up of particles in the belts.

c) If they have sufficient energy, gamma or X-ray radiation may be released on collision with the spacecraft. This may cause ionisation in the body tissues. There may be a cancer risk.

3 a) The constant stream of particles from the Sun.

b) Change its shape.

c) Vast distortions of the magnetic field due to the increased emission of particles.

4 a) See standard text.

b) The direction tells you the sign of the charge carriers.

c) The much higher number density of charge carriers in an ordinary conductor means that the Hall voltage is too small to be useful.

5 0.01 μV.

6 By measuring the Hall voltage produced by a known magnetic field and comparing it with the voltage in an unknown field.

7 The Hall probe gives an electrical signal which can give rise to a signal from the satellite to Earth. It is also small, compact and robust. Old–fashioned magnetometers used the deflection of pivoted magnets like compasses. They were fragile, bulky and needed direct observation.

37 TELEVISION

1 In your discussion try to cite points of agreement and disagreement with the statements given and then draw your conclusions.

2 a) The field will need to be vertically upwards to give a motion from left to right as you look at the screen.

b) $F = Bev = 2 \times 10^{-3} \times 1.6 \times 10^{-19} \times 3 \times 10^{7}$
$= 9.6 \times 10^{-15}$ N.

c) $F = Bev\sin 30 = 4.8 \times 10^{-15}$ N.

3 By changing the p.d. between the cathode and the anode in the electron gun.

4 a) It contains long slits rather than holes.

b) The grid has become magnetised causing deflection of the beams onto the wrong colour spots. The degaussing coil carries an a.c. current which can gradually be reduced to zero as the coil is swept over the screen thus removing the residual field on the grid.

c) No grid needed here.

5 a) (i) Time = 0.04/625 = 6.4×10^{-5} s.

(ii) 25" is the diagonal so take the distance across the screen as approximately 18" = 46 cm. This gives a speed of 7.2×10^{3} m s^{-1}.

b) This assumes an approximate value for the width of the screen and an instantaneous flyback time.

6 See standand texts but you need a saw-toothed graph, i.e. a steadily increasing voltage to drag spot across the screen followed by a rapid decrease.

38 X-RAYS

1 There is only a small change in intensity as X-rays traverse different types of tissue making pictures difficult to interpret. Effects will be more visible with the improved imaging of this technique.

2 a) Maximum energy = $eV_{0} = 1.6 \times 10^{-19} \times 100 \times 10^{3} = 1.6 \times 10^{-14}$ J.

b) Assuming all the energy is transferred to an X-ray photon we get energy of emitted photon = $hf = 1.6 \times 10^{-14}$, giving $f = 2.42 \times 10^{19}$ Hz.

c) $\lambda = c/f$, giving $\lambda = 1.24 \times 10^{-11}$ m.

d) The minimum wavelength will decrease moving the curve to the left.

3 a) They are due to the emission of photons when electrons in the target atoms, excited by the bombardment, fall from a higher to a lower energy level.

b) They stay in the same place as they are characteristic of the target material and not the p.d. across the tube.

c) They will appear at different places as they are characteristic of the difference between energy levels in particular types of atoms.

4 a) This is to spread out the great amount of heat energy that is produced in the target by the bombarding electrons.

b) The tube is evacuated to allow the electron beam to strike the target unimpeded by air molecules. The lead is necessary to protect the operator from scattered X-rays.

5 Glass absorbs X-rays but they can be focused by reflection using a system of curved mirrors.

6 See standard texts on medical physics.

7 Again see standard texts The main principle here is using the X-rays to cause the emission of photoelectrons which are then focussed and concentrated onto a smaller screen.

39 INDUCTION HOBS

1 Some sort of coiled element carrying a.c. is needed to produce a *changing* magnetic flux through the pan base but not a permanent magnet.

2 'It' refers to the pan base which will now be in the changing magnetic field created by the current in the induction coil in the hob. The magnetic field lines will be changing in both size and direction according to the size and direction of the a.c. in the hob coil. The field lines will tend to be concentrated in the base of the pan.

3 Induced currents will flow due to the changes in magnetic flux.

4 If no pan is in place the only induced currents will be in the surrounding material of the hob itself. If this is insulating material little if any secondary induced current will flow leading to little if any current being drawn in the primary induction coil in the hob. With extremely low current flow there will be little heating effect.

5 With stainless steel pans there will be maximum concentration of field lines giving rise to bigger induced currents and faster heating will occur.

6 The presence of air between the pan base and the hob in a local area becomes a problem. Hot spots occur due to the uneven contact and can cause safety cutouts to switch the hob off.

7 a) The eddy currents in the pan base are probably not going to be that of a single loop.

b) (i) 500 W

(ii) $N_s/N_p = V_s/V_p$, therefore $V_s = 20$ V.

(iii) Power $= VI$, gives $I_s = 25$ A.

8 (a) $Z = V/I = 7$ W.

b) $Z = \sqrt{R^2 + (\omega L)^2}$, therefore $L = 1.15 \times 10^{-2}$ H

c) Heating effect $= I^2R = 150 \ \Omega$.

9 The currents are localised in the base and there is no net build-up of charge on the whole pan.

40 INVENTING THE ELECTRIC GENERATOR

1 See the article.

2 In the generator, mechanical energy is being changed to electrical energy. There is no need for an extra injection of electrical energy in the first place.

3 See the article.

4 See the article.

5 a) Faster rotation, greater area of coil, larger number of coils, stronger magnetic field.

b) $E_{max} = BAN\omega = 0.314$ V.

c) See standard text. The coil is parallel to the field.

d) 50 Hz.

6 a) See standard texts and Electricity Generating Company's literature.

   b) (i) The turns ratio is 275:6.

   (ii) Power out = $3000 \times 500 = 1.5$ MW. This is 99% of the power in, therefore power in = 1.515 MW. This gives a current to the supply station of $1.515 \times 10^6 / 11\,000 = 138$ A.

41 ◢ TUNING CIRCUITS

1 When the frequency is high $2\pi fL$ is high, so leading to a high impedance to the high frequency signals and correspondingly a low impedance to the low frequency signals.

2 When the frequency is low $1/2\pi fC$ is high, so leading to a high impedance to the low frequency signals and correspondingly a low impedance to the high frequency signals.

3 See standard text.

4 See standard text.

5 Frequency $= c/\lambda = \dfrac{3 \times 10^8}{1500}$ Hz.

$C = \dfrac{1}{4\pi^2 L f^2}$ giving C as 12.7 μF.

6 a) (i) Peak value $= \sqrt{2} \times 40 = 56.6$ mA.

   (ii) For the coil, $Z^2 = R^2 + (\omega L)^2$, therefore $Z = 22.1\ \Omega$.

   $V_o = I_o Z$, therefore $V_o = 1.25$ V.

   (iii) For the capacitor $Z^2 = \dfrac{1}{(\omega C)^2}$,

   therefore $Z = 31.8\ \Omega$.

   $V_o = I_o Z$, therefore $V_o = 1.8$ V.

   (iv) For the combination, $Z^2 = R^2 + (\omega L - \dfrac{1}{\omega C})^2$,

   therefore $Z = 29.8\ \Omega$.

   $V_o = I_o Z$ therefore $V_o = 1.7$ V.

   b) The potential differences across each component are not in phase with one another.

7 Frequency $= \dfrac{1}{2\pi\sqrt{LC}} = 91.9$ Hz.

42 ◢ IMITATING TRANSFORMERS

1 a) The d.c. is not steady, but a square wave input signal.

   b) The r.m.s. value is $\dfrac{V_P}{\sqrt{2}}$.

2 a) For charging diodes, D_3, D_6 and D_9 act as switches in the off position as do D_{11}, D_8, D_5 and D_2.

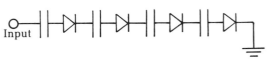

Figure 42.1

For discharging diodes, D_{10}, D_7, D_4 and D_1 act as switches in the off position and diodes D_9, D_6 and D_3 act as open switches drawing the positive charges off the capacitors.

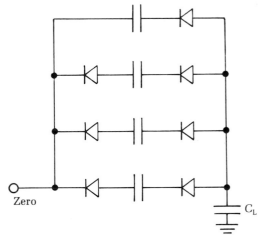

Figure 42.2

   b) See the article. The current source equals the charge on capacitor C_4 over the charge cycle. This is proportional to the potential drop across C_4. The current sink equals charge on C_4 plus charges on C_3, C_2, and C_1 over the discharge cycle.

3 a) If the charge cycle is much longer than the charging time for the capacitors then the maximum p.d. per capacitor is $\dfrac{1}{4}V_P - 0.6$ V when the steady state is reached. (Minimum p.d. to drive a diode = 0.6V.)

For relatively high frequency input and short charging cycles, current flows through the diodes with a consequent voltage drop of V_F across each diode. The charging voltage per capacitor is now

$$\frac{1}{4}V_P - V_F = \frac{1}{4}(V_P - 4V_F).$$

b) When the positive charge has been drained to zero on each capacitor the equivalent negative charge and potential $\frac{1}{4}V_P - V_F$ remains on the other plate. These negative charges cause a flow of positive charge from the load capacitor. For low frequency inputs the discharge cycle is long enough to allow capacitors C_1 ... C_4 to discharge, building a negative charge on the load capacitor and a consequent negative output potential proportional to this charge and to the size of C_L. For high frequency inputs, current flows in D_{11}, D_8, D_5 and D_2 with consequent further drops $-V_F$ from the potential on the negatively–charged plates of capacitors C_1 ... C_4.
Thus, the output potential is approximately

$$-(\frac{1}{4}V_P - V_F) - (-V_F) = -(\frac{1}{4}V_P - 2V_F)$$

c) For a 15 V input and −1.65 V output V_F is calculated from $(15/4) - 2V_F = 1.65$, therefore $V_F = 1.05$ V.
For a 60 V input and −12.9 V output V_F is calculated from $(60/4) - 2V_F = 12.9$, therefore $V_F = 1.05$ V.
For a 28 V input and −5 V output, V_F is calculated from $(28/4) - 2V_F = 5$, therefore $V_F = 1$ V.

4 a) The circuit can be extended as stated by bolting on additional units. The limits arise from heat energy losses through the diodes and more especially an upper theoretical limit occurs when the calculated voltage output is zero or less.

$$-(\frac{1}{n}V_P - 2V_F) \leq 0 \text{, therefore } n \leq \frac{V_P}{2V_F} \text{, where } n \text{ is the}$$

total number of units.
b) There would be a lot of money in it!

43 USING A CAT TO FIND BURIED CABLES

1 a) 50 Hz mains frequency.
b) This is because of the induced currents in them due to the continually changing magnetic flux near a cable carrying a.c. mains.

2 See the article for the origin of this signal. The re-radiation comes about because of the induced a.c. in the buried conductors due to the changing magnetic field caused by the VLF waves.

3 a) Electromagnetic induction.
b) By turning the CAT so that the signal from the search coil is either at a minimum or a maximum, the CAT is either parallel to the conductor or at right angles to it. The maximum induced current in the search coil will occur when there is the greatest rate of change of magnetic flux through the coil.
c) By comparing the signals there is a very narrow directional response pattern established.

4 Possibly by introducing shielding above the coil.

5 a) These include cross-sectional area of search coil, number of turns of search coil, orientation of search coil and distance from the buried cable.
b) Standing waves are developed in the cables. Additional frequencies can be detected.

6 a) $B = \frac{\mu_o I}{2\pi a}$, therefore $B = 2\mu T$

b) e.m.f. $= \frac{200 \times 10 \times 10^{-3}}{0.2} = 10$ V

7 a) Your flow diagram should include input signal, detectors, preamps and filters, comparator, amplifier and loudspeaker.
b) See standard text for the use of an operational amplifier as a voltage comparator.

8

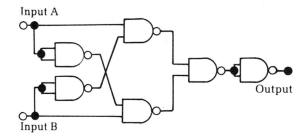

Figure 43.1

44 USING A SIGNAL TO HELP FIND CABLES

1 See article.

2 a) and **b)** See article.

3 If the tone of the signal emitted changes, then the Genny is receiving a signal from the metal cover due to induced currents in the cover which are generated by the changing magnetic field from the Genny signal. This gives positive feedback to the Genny and the resultant combined signal is heard.

4 See standard text.

5 The list is large but will include water mains, gas mains, cable TV, telephone wires and mains electricity cables.

6 a) The r.m.s. current $= \dfrac{10}{\sqrt{2}} = 7.07$ A.

b) The r.m.s. current $= \dfrac{10}{\sqrt{2}} = 7.07$ A.

c) The equivalent d.c. voltage or current that will produce the same heating effect.

MATTER

45 PLAYGROUND PHYSICS

1 a) Gain in potential energy $= mgh$
$= 20 \times 10 \times 3(1 - \cos 30°) = 80.4$ J
b) Maximum kinetic energy = gain in potential energy
$= 80.4$ J

c) $\dfrac{1}{2}mv^2 = 80.4$, therefore $v = 2.84$ m s^{-1}

d) If the maximum tension in each rope of length l is T and it occurs at the bottom of the swing, then

$2T = \dfrac{mv^2}{l} + mg$, therefore $T = 1.27 \times 10^2$ N.

2 a) Maximum stress
$= \dfrac{127}{\pi \times (0.75 \times 10^{-2})^{-2}} = 7.2 \times 10^5$ Pa.

b) Maximum strain $\dfrac{7.2 \times 10^5}{197 \times 10^9} = 3.65 \times 10^{-6}$

c) Maximum extension = 3 × maximum strain
$= 1.1 \times 10^{-5}$ m.
Minimum tension in each rope occurs at the extremity of the swing, so resolving along the ropes, $T = mg\cos 30°/2 = 86.6$ N.

Minimum stress $\dfrac{86.6}{\pi \times (0.75 \times 10^{-2})^{-2}} = 4.9 \times 10^5$ Pa.

Minimum strain $\dfrac{4.9 \times 10^5}{197 \times 10^9} = 2.49 \times 10^{-6}$
Minimum extension = 3 × minimum strain
$= 7.47 \times 10^{-6}$ m.

3 a) and **b)** You will need to consider where (in the swing) forces can be applied to best effect and the best ways in which muscular action can raise the potential energy at the extremes of the swing and the kinetic energy at the low point.

4 a) (i) $\omega = \dfrac{20\pi}{60} = \dfrac{\pi}{3}$ rads^{-1}
Force $= mr\omega^2 = 35 \times 2 \times \dfrac{\pi^2}{9} = 76.8$ N
(ii) If you assume uniform deceleration in 180 s, deceleration

$= \dfrac{\text{maximum tangential speed} - 0}{\text{time taken}}$

$= \dfrac{r\omega - 0}{t} = \dfrac{2\pi/3}{180} = 0.012\, ms^{-2}$

b) As the child goes to the centre, the moment of inertia of the system is reduced and the roundabout will speed up. See standard text.

5 a) The water seems to encourage wet clothing to stick to the slide surface. This may be due to deposits on the metal surface of the slide change in texture when wet.

b) With no friction and using conservation of energy, $v = 7.75$ m s^{-1}.

Energy transfered by friction = force × distance

$$= 10 \times \frac{3}{\sin 30} = 60\,\text{J}$$

$\frac{1}{2}mv^2 = mgh - 60$, therefore $v = 7.5$ m s^{-1}

6 There are an infinite number of possibilities but you need to quote two examples with the clockwise moments about the centre of the see–saw balanced by the anticlockwise moments.

▷ **46   ROPES AND ROCKS**

1 a) Static strength should be measured in N as it is a force. From the catalogue, the static strength = 14 kN or 14.5 kN.

b) (i) Cross–sectional area = $\pi(4.1 \times 10^{-3})^2$
$= 5.28 \times 10^{-5}$ m^2.

Maximum stress $\dfrac{14 \times 10^3}{52.83 \times 10^{-6}}$

$= 2.65 \times 10^8$ Pa.

(ii) Cross–sectional area = $\pi(4.25 \times 10^{-3})^2$
$= 5.68 \times 10^{-5}$ m^2.

Maximum stress $= \dfrac{14.5 \times 10^3}{56.77 \times 10^{-6}} = 2.55 \times 10^8$ Pa.

c) (i) Strain = extension/length = 0.095 for 80 kg

Stress $= \dfrac{800}{52.83 \times 10^{-6}} = 1.51 \times 10^7$ Pa.

Young's modulus = stress/strain = 1.59×10^8 Pa

(ii) Strain = extension/length = 0.075 for 80 kg

Stress $= \dfrac{800}{56.77 \times 10^{-6}} = 1.41 \times 10^7$ Pa.

Young's modulus = stress/strain = 1.88×10^8 Pa.

2 Kinetic energy $E = \frac{1}{2}mv^2$, therefore $(mv)^2 = 2mE$

Thus, momentum of fall $= \sqrt{2mE}$

So, if the impact force is actually an impulsive measure, then it is related to the energy of the fall.

3 The belay point is below the climber. She falls past it. If the rope up to the climber is taut at the moment of fall then the fall factor will be exactly 2. Usually the rope is slack so there is more rope in the system and the fall factor will be less than 2.

4 a) Potential energy lost in initial fall = mgh
= 3000 J.

Further energy loss during extension of Δl metres
= $600\Delta l$ J.

Energy in rope = $0.5\,T\Delta l$, where T = the final tension in N.

$$\frac{T}{800} = \frac{\Delta l/10}{0.075}, \text{ therefore } T = 1067\Delta l \text{ N}.$$

Thus, $3000 = 600\Delta l = \dfrac{1067\Delta l^2}{2} = 533\Delta l^2$

Solving for Δl, extension = 3.00 m.

b) For the Beal rope, the maximum tension T in the rope comes from a fall factor of 2. A force of 800 N gives a stretch of 7.5%.

Let the length of the belay be L and the fall be $2L$ before stretching taut. The energy of fall = $800 \times 2L$ J.

Let the rope stretch a further distance Δl and the energy lost during the further fall = $800\Delta l$ J.

Energy absorbed by the rope during the extension
= $0.5T\Delta l$ J.

Now, $\dfrac{T}{800} = \dfrac{\Delta l/2L}{0.075}$ where T = the maximum tension.

So, $T = 5333(\Delta l/L)$ N, therefore $0.5 \times 5333(\Delta l/L) \times \Delta l$
$= 800\Delta l + 1600L$.

Solving for $\Delta l/L$ gives $\Delta l/L = 0.939$.

Thus, $T = 5335 \times 0.939 = 5.0 \times 10^3$ N.

For the Cousin's rope, a similar analysis gives
$T = 4.56 \times 10^3$ N.

5 If the shaded areas on the graphs are energy and the vertical axis is force, then the horizontal axis can only be extension ΔL. The curiosity is that the curves shown are non–linear which implies a non-Hooke's law situation.

The above analysis comes close to the maximum tension for one of the ropes assuming Hooke's law. The difference might be accounted for in the construction of the rope and the amount by which fibres actually untwist in stretching.

47

APPLYING THE PRESSURE

1 a) See any lock in action or refer to standard text.
b) For every complete cycle of the lock operation a net mass of water falls downstream. This transfers gravitational potential energy into the system.

2 Blood pressure.

3 a) See standard text.
b) They stop working because air is compressible.

4 a) When static you need a force of less than 50 N
b) 20 m.
c) Friction.

5 a) (i) Work done = $1500 \times 10 \times 35 = 5.25 \times 10^5$ J.
(ii) Energy stored = $mgh = 35 \times 200 \times 1000 \times 10 \times (35/2) = 1.23 \times 10^9$ J.
(iii) The same as in (ii) above.
b) Small scale electricity generation?

48

ROCKS AND CRYSTAL STRUCTURES

1 See article.

2 a) and **b)** See article.

3 a) Electron microscope.
b) and **c)** See article and standard text.

4 The increased pressure lowers the melting point of the ice so that it melts at the ambient temperature while under the blade. You are skating on water hence friction is reduced.

5 a) Compressional stress = force per unit area
= weight of rocks above per unit area
= $5500 \times 1000 \times 10 = 55 \times 10^6$ Nm^{-2}.

b) Compressional strain = $\dfrac{55 \times 10^6}{3 \times 10^{11}} = 1.83 \times 10^{-4}$.

49

BALLOONING

1 a) The decrease in the density of the surrounding air at higher altitudes will lead to less upthrust and the cooling of the gas in the balloon will lead to increased density.

b) They are so designed so that the measuring instruments can be recovered and debris from the upper atmosphere removed.
c) (i), (ii) and (iii) In all cases this is to give extra lift due to decreasing the density of the gas which, otherwise, gradually increases due to cooling. You do not want the balloon to go into free fall during descent.

2 a) For hydrogen, weight = $(1.3 - 0.09) \times 10\,000 \times 10$ = 1.21×10^5 N.
b) For helium, weight = $(1.3 - 0.18) \times 10\,000 \times 10$ = 1.12×10^5 N.

3 Force = net upthrust = $(20 \times 1.12 - 10) \times 10 = 124$ N.

4 a) Total mass = $500 \times 0.45 = 225$ kg.
b) Net upward force = net force on the balloon and load including the air inside
= $500 \times 1.2 \times 10 - (0.7 \times 500 + 0.45 \times 500) \times 10$
= $500 \times 0.05 \times 10 = 250$ N.
c) Acceleration = force/total mass
$= \dfrac{250}{(0.7 \times 500) + (45 \times 500)} = 0.43\,\text{ms}^{-2}$.

5 a) 90 kg.
b) 1.14×10^3 m^3.
c) 7.9×10^{-2} kg m^{-3}.
d) Weight = $1.02 \times 1136 \times 10 = 1.16 \times 10^4$ N.

6 a) As in Question 5a).
b) 1.1×10^3 m^3.
c) 8.1×10^{-2} kg m^{-3}.
d) 1.13×10^4 N.

7 a) (i) Root mean square velocity = $(3P/\rho)^{0.5}$
= 480 m s^{-1}.
(ii) 490 m s^{-1}.
b) At a certain height, the root mean square velocity of the gas molecules will be equal to the escape velocity.

50

THERMOMETERS

1 a) It would be affected by the pressure of the atmosphere as well as by temperature.
b) The buoyancy of each glass sphere will depend on the density of the surrounding fluid and the mass and volume of the sphere and weight. Each rises in turn to the top at particular temperatures. Hence, the need for precision weights.

2 a) This is the Fahrenheit scale and the Celsius equivalent is 26–30 °C.
b) This is the Fahrenheit scale and the Celsius equivalent is 36.9 °C.

3 The first equation refers to the relation between the Celsius and Kelvin scales of temperature. The second is an equation to establish any temperature scale in terms of two fixed points.
See any standard text to find out how they are useful.

4 a) It is close to the ideal gas scale. Not in common use as it is bulky and unwieldy.
b) The temperature at which water vapour, water and ice all exist in equilibrium.

5 See standard text for details.

6 a) 79.31 °C
b) No, as different thermometers only correspond at the fixed points.

7 a) and **b)** See standard text.

51 ▶ TREATING SCALDS AND BURNS

1 a) The skin was being cooled by heat flow from the skin to the snow. Heat energy from the skin was absorbed by the snow as latent heat of fusion and some snow melted. The rapid reduction of the temperature of the skin halted the scalding process.
b) Blinking.

2 A sufficient volume needed to be maintained to have an adequate heat sink so the melted snow needed replacing.

3 As the steam condenses on the skin, latent heat of vaporisation is released.

4 a) $0.25 \times 3000 \times (80 - \theta) = 0.5 \times 4200 \times (\theta - 10)$, therefore $\theta = 28.4$ °C.
b) This assumes no heat losses to or from the surroundings including the bowl.
c) To minimise the time for any bacteria to develop in the food.

5 a) Some of the ice would melt.
b) Heat gained by the ice = heat lost by the stew
$m \times 340\,000 = 0.25 \times 3000 \times 80$.
therefore 35.3% of the ice melts.
c) No heat is transferred to or absorbed from the surroundings.

6 a) 3.9×10^4 J and 6×10^4 J.
b) The possibility of freeze burn.
c) The running water continually takes away the heat at a constant rate. With snow you again have the possibility of freeze burn.

52 ▶ A PROBLEM OF SCALE

1 a) These are calcium carbonate or calcium sulphate.
b) A weak acid.
c) Not a good idea to drink the contents (see label).

2 They get clogged up and impede conduction of heat from the water to the room. Closed systems are used with additives in the fluid to prevent build–up of scale.

3 a) (i) $\dfrac{Q}{t} = \dfrac{kA(\theta_1 - \theta_2)}{L}$, therefore

$$3 \times 10^3 = \frac{150 \times \pi \times (0.1)^2 (\theta - \theta_m)}{2.5 \times 10^{-3}} = \frac{1.0 \times \pi (0.1)^2 (\theta_m - 100)}{1.0 \times 10^{-3}}$$

Solving for the temperature of the bottom of the pan $\theta = 197$ °C.
(ii) With no scale, θ works out at 101.6 °C.
b) Obviously the bottom of the pan has to get to a higher temperature before the water boils.

4 a) The graph you draw will be linear with a different gradient across the scale compared to across the metal base.
b) This will be a straight line graph.

5 a) Increase the temperature needed by the base dirt surface to make the water boil.
b) A calculation check along the same lines as Question 3 a) (i) gives a temperature at the dirty base of 165 °C.

53 ▶ INSULATION

1 See article. Radiation, conduction and convection all play a part in the overall picture.

2 See article.

3 Consider all the different means of insulating and draught proofing available.

4 a) (i) W^{-1} m² K
(ii) W m⁻² K⁻¹

b) Let R be the thermal resistance of the whole and R_1, R_2, etc be the thermal resistance of each layer.

Then $R = R_1 + R_2 + R_3$ ... but $R = \dfrac{1}{U}$, therefore

$$\frac{1}{U} = \frac{1}{U_1} + \frac{1}{U_2} + \frac{1}{U_3}$$

5 a) $R = 0.05 + 0.14 + 0.25 + 2(0.3/0.4) = 1.94$ W^{-1} m^2 K.
$U = 1/R = 0.515$ W m^{-2} K^{-1}.
b) $Q/t = 0.515 \times 100 \times 10 = 515$ W.
c) For a single brick, $R = 0.05 + 0.75 + 0.14 = 0.94$ W^{-1} m^2 K. $U = 1/R = 1.06$ W m^{-2} K^{-1}. $Q/t = 1.06 \times 100 \times 10 = 1060$ W, i.e. more than twice as much heat loss.

6 a) $R = 0.05 + 0.14 + 0.15 + (2 \times 0.005) = 0.35$ W^{-1} m^2 K.
$U = 2.86$ W m^{-2} K^{-1}.
b) $Q/t = 2.86 \times 1.0 \times 10 = 28.6$ W.
c) $R = 0.05 + 0.14 + 0.01 = 0.2$ W^{-1} m^2 K.
so $U = 5$ W m^{-2} K^{-1}. $Q/t = 5 \times 1.0 \times 10 = 50$ W, i.e. not quite twice as much heat loss.

7 Here you will need to find out the cost of installation and the subsequent savings leading to a calculation of the payback time and future benefit.

54 USING A MICROWAVE OVEN

1 a) This problem is tackled by using a turntable for the food or rotating antennae to 'stir' the emitted waves.
b) Warm up an array of glasses containing water and monitor the variations in temperature.
c) There are obvious risks if the food does not reach the required temperature to kill germs (recent problems have occured when reheating precooked food).

2 This is done on a timed basis. For a lower setting the magnetron is only switched on for a small percentage of the total time. It is automatically switched on and for repeating time intervals at a particular setting.

3 a) and **b)** If the oven is empty, the magnetron can be damaged by the energy from reflected back microwaves. Metal containers both reflect back the microwaves and can become overheated and distorted in the microwave. In any case the reflections alter the typical pattern for the oven and may cause regions of overheating.

4 Microwaves heat food by causing oscillations of water molecules. We contain a high percentage of water molecules and so microwaves are detrimental to our health.

5 a) Only the outer 4–5 cm will have been heated by the microwaves directly. During the standing time, the heat is being conducted to the centre of the joint which then finishes cooking.
b) Volume of the whole $= 5\pi \times 10^{-4}$ m^3. Volume of the unheated part $= 0.56\pi \times 10^{-4}$ m^3. Volume of the heated part $= 4.44\pi \times 10^{-4}$ m^3. $\Delta Q = mc\Delta\theta$, therefore $4.44\pi \times 10^{-4}(100 - \theta) = 0.56\pi \times 10^{-4}(\theta - 18)$. Solving for the final temperature, $\theta = 90.8°$
c) Some heat energy will be used to boil some of the joint juices, in and just out of the oven, and some conduction may have occurred already within the joint. There will be some heat loss to the room in spite of the foil.

6 The humidity levels rise due to loss of water content in the cooked food. By knowing the type of food and its mass, an estimate can be made of the water content to be detected if the food is cooked. Fat and sugar content can also affect the response to the microwaves.

55 BIOLOGICAL EFFECTS OF RADIATION

1 a) Cosmic rays, rocks and soil, and ingested and inhaled radioactive nuclei.
b) Better detection methods are available. Better home insulation and central heating allows the gas to build up in homes. The gas is emitted from radioactive materials in granite.

2 Changes in DNA can cause genetic problems for future generations.

3 a) If α–producing substances are ingested they will produce the greatest local damage because they have maximum ionising effect. γ–rays are the most penetrating and so can have an effect on tissue deep within the body when the source is outside. However, γ–rays are the least ionising so tissue damage per m of path is less.
b) See the answer to 3 a). This means that special precautions have to be taken not to ingest an α–producing source (e.g. using sealed sources) and using lead shielding to reduce the risk from γ–sources because of their higher penetration.

4 a) Different rocks and soil.

b) Some individuals are more at risk from their jobs, where they live and as a result of medical treatment received.

c) Individuals can monitor how many X-rays are used routinely in medical treatment and can have houses checked if living in a radon gas producing area. If rain is suspect after a nuclear accident such as Chernobyl a good shower after getting wet in the rain can help. However, there is little that can be done overall on a personal basis.

d) They have greater exposure to cosmic radiation.

5 a) See standard text. Include no experiments with sources on a level with your eyes, check sources are all returned to containers at end of experiments, handle sources with tongs pointing away from you.

b) See standard text. Include monitoring dose rate and protective clothing.

6 Photons of γ–radiation carry more energy than photons of infrared radiation.

For a photon of γ–radiation, energy $= hf = hc/\lambda$ $= 6.63 \times 10^{-34} \times 3.0 \times 10^{8}/10^{-15}$, which is approximately $= 2.0 \times 10^{-10}$ J.

For a photon of infrared radiation, energy $= hf$ $= hc/\lambda = 6.63 \times 10^{-34} \times 3.0 \times 10^{8}/10^{-5}$, which is approximately $= 2.0 \times 10^{-20}$ J.

7 See old reports and newspapers - as far as can be gathered from the final report, the rigorous following of standard safety instructions is crucial for nuclear safety.

56 RADIOACTIVE DATING

1 U-235, as the order of one half–life only would have passed.

2 The half–life is too short compared to geological time scales so insufficient measurable amounts of C–14 would be found.

3 $^{14}_{6}C = ^{14}_{7}N + ^{0}_{-1}e + \bar{v}, \quad n = p + e + \bar{v}.$

4 $N = N_0 e^{-\lambda t}$ gives $\ln(N/N_0) = -\lambda t$

But, $\lambda = \ln2/5730$, so $t = \dfrac{\ln0.78 \times 5730}{\ln 2} = 2.05 \times 10^{3}$ a.

5 $t = -\ln(\dfrac{8.4}{15.2}) \times \dfrac{5730}{\ln 2} = 4.90 \times 10^{3}$ a.

6 a) Assuming no lead–207 was present initially in the rock but that it is all due to the decay of the U–235, 32 lots of U–235 have become 1 lot of U–235. $32 = 2^5$, so five half–lives have passed.

b) The rock is $5 \times 704 = 3.52 \times 10^{3}$ Ma old.

7 If the number of half–lives $= n$ then $2^n = 11$, giving $n = \ln11/\ln2$. The age of the rock $= 48\,800 \times \ln11/\ln2 = 1.69 \times 10^{5}$ Ma.

8 The cannon balls are likely to be free of the radioactive isotope and so provide useful shields which do not add to the radioactivity detected.

57 SMOKE DETECTORS

1 α–particles produce the highest number of ion pairs per cm of track compared to β– and γ– emissions.

2 Because of the answer to Question 1, α– sources are dangerous if ingested.

3 Relatively short half–life and weak.

4 Assuming that the ionisation current is due to the positive and negative ions created, the current $= 1500 \times 5.2 \times 10^{4} \times 1.6 \times 10^{-19} = 1.25 \times 10^{-11}$ A

5 a) $\lambda = \ln2/(4 \times 365 \times 24 \times 3600) = 5.49 \times 10^{-9}$ s^{-1}. Activity $= -dN/dt = \lambda N = 5.49 \times 10^{-9} \times 10^{12} = 5490$ Bq^{-1}

b) Fraction remaining after one year $= N/N_0 = e^{-\lambda t} = \exp(-5.49 \times 10^{-9} \times 365 \times 24 \times 60 \times 60) = 0.841$.

c) Activity $= \lambda N = 5.49 \times 10^{-9} \times 0.841 \times 10^{12} = 4617$ Bq^{-1}

d) Maximum ionisation current $= 4617 \times 5.2 \times 10^{4} \times 1.6 \times 10^{-19} = 3.85 \times 10^{-11}$A.

6 a) Possibly the reduction of the range of α–particles, caused by collisions with smoke particles reduces the number of ions generated.

b), c) and **d)** See standard text for various possibilities.

7 Possibly the presence of a small quantity of smoke causes a bigger change in the effectiveness of the photoelectric detector than in the ionisation current.

8 See standard text. The current in the photocell will be reduced if smoke interrupts the light beam that falls onto the cell.

58 ▶ FLUORESCENT LAMPS

1 Line spectra are due to excited electrons at higher energy levels falling to lower energy levels and giving out photons of energy equal to the difference between the energy levels.

2 They emitted light of a single frequency rather than a range of frequencies. This meant that the frequencies needed for us to observe all colours other than this particular yellow were missing.

3 The light tended not to be scattered as much by fog particles as a light from a higher or mixed frequency source.

4 The coatings contained materials with electron energy levels such that an excited electron could lose its energy by a series of jumps down the levels giving rise to different frequency photons being emitted.

5 a) Photon energies = hc/λ giving 3.03 × 10⁻¹⁹ J, 4.09 × 10⁻¹⁹ J, 4.58 × 10⁻¹⁹ J, and 4.85 × 10⁻¹⁹ J.
b) The photon energies in eV are 1.90, 2.55, 2.86, and 3.03, so the next four energy levels will be 12.1 eV, 12.8 eV, 13.1 eV and 13.2 eV.

6 a) Photon energy = hc/λ giving 3.37 × 10⁻¹⁹ J

$$= \frac{3.37 \times 10^{-19}}{1.60 \times 10^{-19}} \text{ eV} = 2.1 \text{ eV}.$$

b) Electric field strength = V/d = 2.1/1.0 × 10⁻⁴ = 2.1 × 10⁴ V m⁻¹.
c) Higher pressure will give a shorter mean distance between molecules so a higher field strength will be needed.

7 a) Energy transformed by the Wotan bulb
= 11 × 4 × 3 600 × 7 = 1.11 MJ.
Energy transformed by the ordinary bulb
= 60 × 4 × 3 600 × 7 = 6.05 MJ.
Energy saved = 4.94 MJ.
b) Heat losses from a filament lamp are eliminated using a fluorescent tube.

59 ▶ RADIATION PRESSURE FROM THE SUN

1 a) (i) Change of momentum = $-h/\lambda$
(ii) Change of momentum = $-(h/\lambda) - (h/\lambda) = -2h/\lambda$
b) Impulse in (i) = h/λ and the impulse in (ii) = $2h/\lambda$

2 In **a)** (i) the change of momentum s⁻¹ m⁻² = nh/λ
In **a)** (ii) the change of momentum s⁻¹ m⁻² = $2nh/\lambda$

3 a) (i) Pressure = nh/λ
(ii) Pressure = $2nh/\lambda$
b) Units check gives s⁻¹ m⁻² Js m⁻¹ = m⁻² Nm m⁻¹ = Nm⁻² = Pa.

4 New pressure = $2nh \cos60/\lambda = nh/\lambda$

5 a) Total number of photons per second = 60/energy of one photon.
Energy of one photon = $hf = hc/\lambda$

$$= \frac{6.63 \times 10^{-34} \times 3 \times 10^8}{590 \times 10^{-9}}$$
= 3.37 × 10⁻¹⁹ J.
So, the total number of photons per second
= 60/3.37 × 10⁻¹⁹ = 1.78 × 10²⁰.
b) The total number is spread over surface of a sphere of area = $4\pi r^2$ giving the number incident per second per square metre

$$= \frac{1.78 \times 10^{20}}{4\pi(0.5)^2}$$
= 5.67 × 10¹⁹.

c) Pressure $= \frac{2nh}{\lambda} = \frac{2 \times 5.67 \times 10^{19} \times 6.63 \times 10^{-34}}{590 \times 10^{-9}}$

= 1.27 × 10⁻⁷ Pa.

6 You use the particle model when light interacts with a surface. You use the wave model for the transmission of light.

7 The pressure is inversely proportional to the square of the distance from the source so the pressure would be quadrupled.

60 ► BURGLAR ALARMS

1 a) The current will increase to a maximum value.

b) As the voltage is increased the current observed will decrease to zero. This will occur at the stopping voltage V_s when $eV_s = hf - hf_o$ and the emitted electrons are just attracted back again to the cathode.

2 a) Maximum energy = 3.6 −2.8 = 0.8 eV.

b) 0.8 V.

3 a) See standard text.

b) $hf_o = 3$ eV giving $f_o = \dfrac{3 \times 1.6 \times 10^{-19}}{6.63 \times 10^{-34}} = 7.2 \times 10^{14}$ Hz.

Infrared radiation frequencies are less than this and so would not cause any photoelectric emission.

4 See standard text.

5 a) Photon energy = 4.3 eV = 6.88×10^{-19} J.

b) $hf = 6.88 \times 10^{-19}$, therefore $f = 1.04 \times 10^{15}$ Hz.

c) Number of photoelectrons emitted per second

$= \dfrac{0.005 \times 10^{-3}}{1.6 \times 10^{-19}} = 3.1 \times 10^{13}$.

d) The threshold frequency $= \dfrac{2.8 \times 1.6 \times 10^{-19}}{6.63 \times 10^{-34}}$

$= 0.68 \times 10^{15}$ Hz.

6 Measurements of the stopping voltage, V_s, when a photocathode is illuminated with radiation of different frequencies. The gradient of a graph of V_s against f would be a straight line of slope = h/e.